HEAD AND HAND IN ANCIENT GREECE

FOUR STUDIES IN THE
SOCIAL RELATIONS OF THOUGHT

By the same Author

SCIENCE AND POLITICS IN THE ANCIENT WORLD
SCIENCE IN ANTIQUITY
GREEK SCIENCE: ITS MEANING FOR US (available from Spokesman)

HEAD AND HAND IN ANCIENT GREECE

FOUR STUDIES IN THE SOCIAL
RELATIONS OF THOUGHT

BY
BENJAMIN FARRINGTON

*With a new Foreword by
Barry Baldwin*

SPOKESMAN

First published in the Thinker's Library in 1947, by the Rationalist Press Association, 47 Theobalds Road, London WC1X 8SP
This edition published in 2001 by agreement.

Spokesman
Russell House
Bulwell Lane, Nottingham NG6 0BT
Phone 0115 9708318
Fax 0115 9420433
e-mail elfeuro@compuserve.com
©2001 Estate of Benjamin Farrington

All rights reserved. No part of this book may be reprinted or reproduced or utilised in any form or by any electronic, mechanical, or other means, now known or hereafter invented, including photocopying and recording, or in any information storage or retrieval system, without permission in writing from the publishers.

ISBN 0 85124 654 0

A CIP catalogue record is available form the British Library

Printed by the Russell Press Ltd. (phone 0115 9784505)

CONTENTS

		PAGE
FOREWORD		
PREFACE		
INTRODUCTION		
I.	THE CHARACTER OF EARLY GREEK SCIENCE	1
II	THE HAND IN HEALING: A STUDY IN GREEK MEDICINE FROM HIPPOCRATES TO RAMAZZINI	28
III	DIODORUS SICULUS: UNIVERSAL HISTORIAN	55
IV	THE GODS OF EPICURUS AND THE ROMAN STATE	88

ACKNOWLEDGMENTS

Two of these papers, *The Character of Early Greek Science* and *The Hand in Healing*, were first read at The Royal Institution of Great Britain. *Diodorus Siculus* was the Inaugural Lecture given by the author when he became Professor of Classics at Swansea. The paper on *The Gods of Epicurus and the Roman State* first appeared in The Modern Quarterly.

FOREWORD

To adapt a Latin adverb-illustrating sentence we were given at school, I once met Benjamin Farrington but I only met him once. In a group of hangers-on, at some conference or other. He was more attentively courteous to a humble undergraduate than would have been the usual godlike professor of those far-off days.

Irish affability? Born on 10 July 1891 (eight years after Marx' death), Farrington read classics at University College in his native Cork, then Trinity College, Dublin – I expect he savoured Joyce's *Ulysses* epigram: 'Trinity medicals, all prick and no pence.' Then a hat-trick of sorts, getting his foot on the academic ladder with an assistant lectureship at Queen's University, Belfast, in 1916, year of the Easter Uprising.

Two other distinguished Marxist ancient historians shared these Irish connections: Edward Thompson (my Nottingham professor in the fifties) and George Thomson at Birmingham. Regarding this difference in name-spelling, George once remarked, 'Edward took the "pee" out of me.' Perhaps another reason why he sometimes styled himself Seoirse Mac Laghmainn.

As his pupil, encountering Thompson in left-wing politics posed a very English problem: how to address him in these egalitarian circles? 'Professor' seemed wrong, 'Comrade' unthinkable: the matter lacked resolution. Edward made his own the late Roman Empire (some affected to believe he invented it), in a flow of articles and books, most memorably on Attila the Hun. They are lavishly praised by Perry Anderson in *Passages from Antiquity to Feudalism* (1974). Appropriately, Edward's last book was a splendidly irreverent biography of St Patrick.

Twelve years younger than Farrington, English-born George Thomson went from Dulwich College (P. G. Wodehouse was a coeval there) to King's College, Cambridge. An Irish grandfather sparked his interest in that language, into which he translated authors from Aeschylus to Augustine. The preface to his

FOREWORD

Aeschylus and Athens (1941) honours 'my friends the peasant-fishermen of the Blasket Island in West Kerry, who taught me among many things that could not have been learnt from books, what it is like to live in a pre-capitalist society.' In 1931, Thomson was appointed 'Lecturer in Greek through Irish' at Galway, doubtless partly attracted by its 'godless college' reputation. His abrupt departure in 1934 remains a mystery, but is plausibly linked to official dislike of his politics – he would join the British Communist Party the next year. People still take potshots at him, most recently (2000) the ever-snide Mary Beard ((*The Invention of Jane Harrison*) for writing 'a fulsomely hagiographic and sadly apolitical' introduction to his mother-in-law Jane Stewart's biography of the controversial classicist-anthropologist Jane Harrison. In fact, his praise was genuine: *Aeschylus and Athens* admiringly acknowledges her investigations into primitive religion.

In 1920, meanwhile, Farrington had made a more geographically dramatic move to South Africa, where over the next fifteen years at Cape Town he would rise (albeit not without trace, as Kitty Muggeridge said of David Frost) from lecturer to chair in classics. He was as drawn to that country's native cultures as was Thomson to Irish fisherfolk and Thompson to Huns and Visigoths, translating early Latin accounts of indigenous South Africans.

In 1946, with both men back in Britain, there was a confluence of these interests when Farrington wrote the introduction to Thomson's booket *Marxism and Poetry*, which explores the origin and evolution of poetry through its achievements in English, Greek, and Irish. This comparative approach, stemming from Marx himself – admirably documented in S. S. Prawer's *Karl Marx and World Literature* 1976) – and not forgetting Trotsky's *Literature and Revolution*, is early manifest in Farrington's translations of the Latin medical writings of Boerhaave and Vesalius.

Farrington had left South Africa in 1935, briefly in self-demotion to a lectureship at Bristol, a university that owes as much to smoking as does Nottingham to pharmacy ('Jesse Boot dispensing wisdom,' as D. H. Lawrence gibed), then a final re-Celtification in the chair at University College, Swansea, occupied until retirement in 1956 (the year of Suez and Hungary), after which he ended up in Lymington, Hampshire, dying on 17 November 1974.

During Farrington's time at Swansea, its most famous-to-be young lecturer was Kingsley Amis. The firebrand of *Lucky Jim*, not the Evelyn Waugh clone of later years. There is no direct mention of Farrington in the Swansea chapter of Amis' *Memoirs*, nor in Zachary Leader's recent edition of his *Letters*. He was certainly not the model for Professor Welch. But Amis followed his department through sharing digs with Willie Smythe, 'an eccentric Irish Latinist', his Latin 'putting him rather on his own in a classics department full of Graecists and, within a few years, under a professor who favoured teaching the classics in translation.' While Farrington could crudely be labelled a Graecist, the dichotomy does not suit one who ranged from Homer through Lucretius and Rome to late antiquity to Bacon, Butler, and Darwin. And, by implication, his pedagogy was preferable to his translation-preferring successor, not that Farrington scorned any way of sharing the classics – his 'popular' books *Science in Antiquity* and *The Civilisation of Greece and Rome* show that. In his turn, what did Farrington make of Amis' letter in the *Daily Worker* of 14 February 1957 (a poisoned Valentine, indeed) taking exception to Marxist Arnold Kettle's *favourable* review of his *Socialism and the Intellectuals*?

He was lucky enough to miss the newfangled 'research assessments', but Farrington's output would have satisfied the most purblind apparatchik. Apart from *Head and Hand*, the most enduring books are *Primum Graius Homo* (echoing Lucretius' tribute to Epicurus), *Greek Science: Its Meaning for Us* (the sub-title characterising his approach), *Science and Politics in the Ancient World* (Marx would have approved that title), along with those on Francis Bacon and Charles Darwin.

Horace hoped that in his poetry he had 'built myself a monument more lasting than bronze' through which 'I shall never completely die.' Farrington's books continue to be reprinted and raved both over and against. Internet users need only type in his name to get hundreds of references ranging from a Finnish translation of *What Darwin Really Said* to this introductory paean by the relevantly distinguished Joseph Needham to a new edition of *Greek Science*: 'Anyone who wants a rattling good introduction to the development of Greek science set against its

FOREWORD

social background can have no better guide than Benjamin Farrington.'

In these days of academic Newspeak, 'rattling good' is a tribute earned equally by style and content. *Head and Hand* is a particularly readable example of Farrington's limpid prose, a no-nonsense English that is – well, classical: I think here also of Wodehouse who blessed the Greek and Latin verses he had to write at Dulwich, and Raymond Chandler who thanked his classical training there for the lapidary epigrams of his Philip Marlowe novels.

At a UNESCO-sponsored conference commemorating Marx' death centenary in 1983, veteran warhorse Eric Hobsbawm cheekily asked What is a Marxist Historian? Supplying his own answer, Hobsbawm concluded that the extent of Marxist influence is best measured by the fact that, unless advertised, it is not always possible to tell the difference between Marxist and non-Marxist.

For some, both rival academics and those odd birds who 'post' their rantings on the Internet, Farrington's politics are a problem and a pity. I waste no time on them. Reception by other Marxists is more germane. As the Roman grammarian Terentianus Maurus said, *'habent sua fata libelli'* – books have their own destinies. Ignored (as was George Thomson) by Perry Anderson, Farrington was extolled in my former colleague Alban Winspear's *Lucretius and Scientific Thought* (1963). Academic Marxists are (of course) as spitefully internecine as Trotskyite groupuscules. Thus, Geoffrey De Ste. Croix in his Brobdingnagian (authors should remember that to be immortal you don't have to be eternal) *The Class Struggle in the Ancient Greek World* (1981) in an unindexed passage (p. 541 n1) condescendingly remarks 'Benjamin Farrington has also made use of Marxist concepts,' while Robert Padgug in the American classical journal *Arethusa*'s 1975 special issue *Marxism and the Classics* dismisses his approach as 'a somewhat vulgar Marxist one.'

George Thomson gets the same mixed treatment. For Padgug his *Prehistoric Aegean* (3rd ed. 1961) provides 'the most satisfactory study of early Greek communal society'; to Ste. Croix, Thomson's ('not a historian in the proper sense') continuing account in *The First Philosophers* (1955) – a book now remarkable-looking for its lavish quotations from Stalin – is 'little better than fantasy.'

FOREWORD

I don't see Marx and Engels in *Head and Hand*. But Farrington's sympathies are once paraded, in the paper on Greek medicine: 'the USSR is the only country so far that has solved the problem of providing adequate medical attention for the whole of its working population. And the Moscow Hospital for Industrial Diseases is the only one of its kind.' These remarks pre-date the National Health Service.

In *Greek Science*, Marx is linked with Hegel for having 'deepened and developed the ideas of Vico and Francis Bacon until they have become precious tools for man by which he may consciously labour at the amelioration of his own society. In the light of these conceptions, the history of science assumes a new importance.'

Engels here also receives high praise, for his insights into slavery and technology in *Origin of the Family*. Not surprisingly in a series dedicated to Marx' memory, Farrington flies his colours most redly when introducing Thomson's *Marxism and Poetry*: 'These essays, written by Marxists, are a contribution to the creation of confidence among men in their ability to control their own destiny... Marxism provides an extraordinarily powerful instrument of analysis.'

Head and Hand comprises four papers. Such collections are not always worthwhile, but this one preserves three otherwise fugitive pieces (Farrington's Swansea inaugural lecture and two addresses to The Royal Institution of Great Britain) and one published in *The Modern Quarterly* (1938) where many classicists no doubt missed it the first time round.

Reserving the first paper, I jump to the others. The second assesses ancient medicine, with much comparative material from Ramazzini and Vesalius. Farrington would be glad that modern medicine now gives Hippocrates credit for realising the astonishing curative powers of aspirin. Apropos human dissection, he might welcome this morbid addition from the Byzantine chronicler Theophanes on the fate of a religious heretic: 'His hands and feet were cut off, then though he still lived, a physician cut him open from pubis to chest to study human anatomy, after which he was burnt alive.' Farrington's finale was over-generous: 'As such, the doctor constituted the sanest and noblest figure of classical antiquity.' Lest we enviously compare these paragons with the Harold Shipmans of our time, this was not how the Greeks and Romans saw them. Doctor jokes abound in classical literature. Pliny's *Natural History* describes the profession in terms of money-grubbing, quackery, and quarrelling 'like philosophers.' Athenaeus (c. AD 200) crushingly summarised: 'Were it not for doctors, there wouldn't be anything stupider than professors' – Ouch! Marx, who doubtless saw too much of physicians with his piles, would have smiled at Ste. Croix's classification of them with whores and 'other providers of essential services.'

In his 1937 Swansea Inaugural, Farrington does his best for Diodorus Siculus, whose *Universal History* (a genre understandably at low ebb since H. G. Wells) is nowadays more rubbished than read. No one would call Diodorus first-class, and Farrington doesn't strain after gnats, though he shows how faddish are literary reputations by describing the huge esteem in which he was held by his seventeenth-century translators Henry Cogan and George Booth. The virtue Farrington finds in Diodorus is compassion, manifest in his horrifying accounts of miners' sufferings that would strike all too loud a chord with their modern counterparts, as would the ancient anticipation of the Davy lamp. Fronto complained there was no word for pity in Latin, which had to borrow the Greek one – overstating the case, but there was a case to be overstated. Ste. Croix follows suit: 'He shows some signs – exceptional in a Greek or Roman writer – of sympathising with the oppressed.' Diodorus is not in Prawer's inventory of Marx' classical sources. Farrington is also one of the few English writers to read Robert von Pohlman's 's *Geschichte der sozialen Frage und des Sozialismus in der antiken Welt* (3rd ed. 1925) – not in Ste. Croix' bibliography or index.

The best commentary on 'The Gods of Epicurus and the Roman State' is Farrington's own *Science and Politics in the Ancient World*, of which it is the trailer. Notably absent from the discussion is Marx himself, for whom Epicurus was '*der grosste griechische Aufklarer*' (greatest of the Greek Enlighteners) and whose doctoral thesis on the atomic theories of Democritus and Epicurus is lavishly praised (*Classical Quarterly* 22, 1928) by the distinctly non-Marxist Lucretian Cyril Bailey for its 'illuminating ideas.' For Farrington, 'the dominant fact is that it was the Government itself that was the great purveyor of superstition in ancient Rome.' He assembles the quotations from Polybius,

FOREWORD

Cicero, and Augustine that have become standard props, to which I add Ovid's poetic quip *'expedit esse deos'* (useful things, gods) – religion is already the opium of the people. Thus, Epicurus and Lucretius were subverted into moral and political menaces by 'Establishment' writers. As Farrington rightly stresses, Epicurus was not an atheist, despite ancient slurs that with equal absurdity tarred the Christians with this same brush – the two sects once united in a remarkable Popular Front against Alexander of Abonoteichus, a religious charlatan of the kind that pullulate on American television. There was in fact strikingly little ancient atheism, something Farrington might have further explored – the word is not in his *Science and Politics in the Ancient World* index, though other relevant -isms are. The (to us) obscure Diagoras was prosecuted for atheism in democratic Athens, while Protagoras' aphorism Man Is the Measure of All Things suggests a demotion of the divine. By positing gods that have no concern for human affairs, Epicurus and Lucretius were pre-figuring seventeenth-century Deism. Their other 'subversive' teaching was that good people should eschew politics and 'drop out' of society to live in tranquil obscurity. This ultimately selfish creed was a challenge to the Athenian notion that civic involvement is a duty and a man who avoids politics an 'idiot' – nowadays, most people think the opposite. Farrington might here have spotlighted one exception: along with the Stoic Brutus it was the Epicurean Cassius who orchestrated the Ides of March – an intriguing alliance, a pre-Marxist example old and rare of philosophers proceeding from explaining the world to changing it.

In a Desert Island Discourses choice, I'd take the first, in which Farrington surveys the early Ionian philosopher-scientists' god-free explanations of Nature's origin and workings. He rightly eschews the traditional 'Pre-Socratic' label which gives the misleading impression that they were mere warm-ups to the main act. In my opinion (partly shared by Farrington in chapter six of *Greek Science*), Socrates would have been a good turn on a Hyde Park Corner soap-box, otherwise he was an over-inflated windbag, the ancient Isaiah Berlin (adroitly deflated by Christopher Hitchens – see the republished version in *Unacknowledged Legislation: Writers in the Public Sphere*, 2001).

Why should Miletus produce so many of these early thinkers?

FOREWORD

Farrington points to the cultural-geographical factors – contact with the older Eastern civilisations, thus anticipating the current kerfuffle over Martin Bernal's *Black Athena*. But it remains at least diverting that Thales and company should hail from a city otherwise famous for dyes, double-beds, and dildos – as though Los Angeles had pioneered American science.

A masterly analysis of Lucretius shows that what was thought a passage of pure poetry actually betrays keen scientific insight, e.g. the effect of winds on the sea. Farrington would return to Lucretius in a 1965 book on him, edited (ironically) by D. R. Dudley, High Tory colleague of George Thomson. Farrington's argument was taken up in 1974 by the non-Marxist Peter Wiseman who inferred from technical allusions that Lucretius 'worked for his living at more than one trade and saw Rome from a good way below the top of the social ladder,' adding the corollary that his poem was addressed to the man in the Roman street.

As usual with Farrington, there is lavish quoting and praise of Francis Bacon, to whom he devoted two books. Marx himself frequently adduced him, both in *Kapital* and his letters, e.g. *The Reign of King Henry VII* on the link between prosperous peasantry and efficient infantry. Otherwise, through Marxian 'bookworming', Farrington ranges from Aeschylus (a predictable debt to Thomson) and Aristotle ('closer to Marx than any other ancient thinker' – Ste. Croix) to Tolstoy.

Quoting Bacon on prejudice against the mechanical arts led Farrington towards – he would go further in *Greek Science* – THE question: was ancient science/technology fatally impeded by slavery? Marxist and quasi-Marxist luminaries taking this view include Perry Anderson ('the stifling effects of slavery on technique'), J. D. Bernal (*Science in History*), F. W. Walbank (*The Awful Revolution*), and Edward Thompson in his edition of the anonymous late Roman weapons inventor – apparently never used but known through the illustrated editions to Leonardo da Vinci. Ste. Croix, however, disavowed the connection, likewise David Konstan on Marxism and Ancient Slavery in the *Arethusa* supplement. Both for the same reason, in almost identical language: 'I myself know of nothing in Marx to justify the belief that he thought slavery necessarily a hindrance to technical progress' – Ste. Croix' version.

FOREWORD

The debate continues, not only between Marxists. David Keys in the *Independent on Sunday*, 24 January 1993, ventures: 'The Romans would have been capable of an industrial revolution, had their social and economic circumstances required one. Embryonic technology existed to build steamships, trains, mechanically-powered looms, even complex computers. So why did Rome never make the breakthrough?'

A bit febrile, but Keys is going the right way. Ancient technology was much better than commonly alleged. Discovery of fire and the wheel were single-event industrial revolutions. Chaldeans pioneered astronomy and mathematics. Egyptians built pyramids and trepanned brains. The Phaistos Disc with its 48 characters impressed into wet clay can be (indeed, has been) seen as a Bronze Age near-miss in printing. Thompson's inventor's paddle-wheel marks the first belief that ships could move without oars or sails; his artillery devices pioneeringly abandoned the traditional principle of torsion. Theodoric the Gothic King of Italy asked Boethius to design a sundial and a clock for indoors and rainy days. That these were beyond the savant's skills does not make the royal requests any less interesting. Anyway, before the developments chronicled in Jean Gimpel's *La Révolution Industrielle du Moyen Age* (1976) Lucian describes an alarm-clock and Procopius of Gaza a kind of cuckoo-clock on which Hercules hourly went through his Twelve Labours.

Except for occasional gluts in the market, slaves were not cheap to buy, and they were expensive to maintain in good working order. Nor did slavery eliminate the free working and peasant classes. Hence, there was incentive to cut costs by technological advance. Aristotle (*Politics* 1, 4, 1253b) comments that if shuttles and plectra could be automated, masters would not need slaves nor industrialists workers – no suggestion that slavery blocked mechanisation.

Two Roman anecdotes concern suppression of inventions. The emperor Tiberius executed an inventor of unbreakable glass to hush up his discovery. Film fans will recognise a precursor of Alec Guinness' *Man in the White Suit*. Individual inventive spirit is manifest; it is equally significant that the poor fellow was expecting a reward. The emperor Vespasian paid an engineer a handsome reward to hush up his discovery of a cheap transport method for heavy building materials, explaining that he 'must feed his poor people.' Historians of all stripes puzzle over this tale; Ste. Croix was not justified in blithely dismissing it as a fabrication.

With his eagle eye Marx (*Kapital*, book one) spotted a *Greek Anthology* poem (9. 418) describing a water-mill by the inconsequential versifier Antipater (1st cent. BC). Half the epigram describes its technology, in matter-of-fact Greek and unastonished tones. The opening couplet tells slave-girls they can sleep in, their work being done for them; the closing one rejoices that such devices permit a return to primitive ease. Marx saw in this water-mill 'an invention that is the elementary form of all machinery,' followed by William Morris in 'Art under Plutocracy'. The poem provoked Marx to one of his astutest points: 'Oh, those heathens! They did not comprehend that machinery is the surest means of lengthening the working day' – our age of computers and e-mail has painfully vindicated this!!

The architect Vitruvius had already blue-printed the water-mill with no suggestion that it was either novelty or toy. Pliny says the greater part of Italy used it. Or, tried to. The water-mill ushered in no industrial revolution. Bernal pointed out one mundane reason: Italy's quiet rivers and streams did not always suit their use.

Keys also rejects the slavery explanation, preferring to blame the anti-business attitudes of ancient aristocrats, also a traditional view, one with which Farrington flirted. It will not work as a catch-all solution. The anti-banausic sneers of (say) Plato and Cicero no more imply collective classical scorn than the anti-trade snobberies in White's Club. Ste. Croix proves with a wealth of texts that 'to say the ancient Greeks despised craftsmen is one of those deeply misleading statements which show blindness to the existence of all but the propertied Few.'

Ancient technology is full of 'one-offs' (e.g. Byzantine robot servants, domestic steam power, a new hydraulic device, self-refilling lamps, even a tavern with ejector-floor for patrons), gadgets that never entered everyday life. Perhaps ancient brains suffered from what Tom Wilkie (*British Science and Politics since 1945*, 1991) dubs 'a prevailing British disease: the British are good at inventing things but poor at turning them into products to buy.' Be that as it may, two basic questions remain unanswered by all: why did it take so long after slavery for the

FOREWORD

Industrial Revolution to happen? How could it happen in an age abounding in cheap wage slaves?

Wilkie's remark allows me a concluding coda. Farrington assembled *Head and Hand* in 1946, the year of his overtly ideological introduction to *Marxism and Poetry*. The previous year, at Herbert Morrison's request, a 'Memorandum on the Need for a Central Government Science Secretariat' was drafted by the two men who had whipped up the Penguin Special *Science in War* in 1940: Solly Zuckerman (see his 1988 memoir *From Apes to Warlords*, plus Peter Hennessy's *Never Again: Britain 1945-51*, 1993) and the Marxist crystallographer J. D. Bernal.

This Memorandum began: 'The economic condition of Britain today demands the fullest use and extension of our scientific resources in the restoration of industry and agriculture, and in the development of the social services – which in turn calls for a large measure of forward-looking thinking and bold and energetic planning.'

Thanks to government inertia (doubtless exacerbated by Attlee-Morrison feuds), the Memorandum came to nothing, but these words would have been echoed by the acknowledged mentors of Bernal's *Science in History* (whose own introduction restates them): Gordon Childe, Maurice Cornforth, R. Palme Dutt, Christopher Hill, George Thomson – and Benjamin Farrington!

Barry Baldwin, Calgary, May 2001

PREFACE

HERE are four essays which treat four great movements of ancient thought historically—that is, in close relation to their social setting. If there be anything true in them they should help us to see beneath the surface of the social phenomena of our own day.

The first discusses the character of the great early period of Greek science and shows that, while it was not yet experimental, neither was it purely speculative. It was, in fact, closely related to practice. The Ionian philosophers were not simply observers of nature but active interferers with nature, for the philosopher and the man of action were yet one. They made a distinction between necessity and design—that is, between the spontaneous processes of nature and the action of man on nature. They attempted to understand the spontaneous processes of nature—the realm of necessity—in the light of the controlled processes—the realm of design. Thus, though experimental research had not yet been developed, speculation was controlled by being related to experience.

The second essay traces the effect on the art and science of medicine of social changes affecting the attitude to manual work and the manual worker. It claims that the Hippocratic doctors, rightly famous for their analysis of the patient as a living organism striving to maintain itself in balance with its environment, yet overlooked the chief factor in a human being's environment—his job. It is through his job

PREFACE

that society chiefly acts on the individual. If the individual is failing to react adequately to his environment, very often it is his working conditions that need alteration.

Stoicism forms the subject of the third essay, Stoicism as a living and developing movement in a changing environment. Looking through the eyes of the historian Diodorus Siculus we can see Stoicism as a way of life largely eastern in origin. It was at first inspired by astrological beliefs in a just society and was critical of the social injustices of Greek society. Later it declined into being the social cement of the Roman State and a school of resignation.

The Roman State, aided by Stoicism, made as much use as it could of religion as a means of policing society. The fourth and last essay shows how the mild religion and bold science of Epicurus, the rapid spread of which throughout Italy threatened to rob superstition of its police function, alarmed the governing class at Rome and produced an intellectual battle in which the statesman Cicero and the poet Lucretius were on opposite sides.

B. F.

Swansea,
    September 21, 1946.

INTRODUCTION

It is agreed on all hands that the Greeks were great thinkers. Let nobody suppose I wish to dispute this fact. But it is widely taught that the Greeks were poor doers as well as great thinkers. I do wish to dispute this belief. I do wish to assert that the best Greek thinking was the companion and helper of vigorous action.

Nowadays bookish people have lost the sense for all the intellect that exists outside books. A farm, a factory, an engine, a ship, the back-axle of a motor-car, a wheel-barrow, a fishing-rod, is not seen as an intellectual achievement. No. The philosopher sits in his study and murmurs

> My days among the dead are passed.
> Around me I behold,
> Where'er these casual eyes are cast,
> The mighty minds of old.

The mighty minds are all between covers, and I do not deny that some of the ancient Greeks shared the same illusion. But not all. Not Aeschylus, whose *Prometheus* catalogues in such picturesque detail all the crafts he taught to men. Not Sophocles, who celebrates the incredible ingenuity of man's technical inventiveness. Not Herodotus, who gives the island of Samos a special chapter in his history because it was the site of three great feats of engineering. Not Xenophon, who has left us an enthusiastic description of the varied equipment and exquisite order of a Phoenician ship. Not the Hippocratic doctors, whose

INTRODUCTION

disciplined manual skill was the basis of so much of their successful practice. Not Anaxagoras, who saw that the hand had played a decisive part in the development of man from the beast.

Feeling that the active element in Greek science still lacks emphasis in comparison with the contemplative, I have thought it worth while to look for a larger audience for these papers than those to which they were in the first instance addressed.

Since these pages were first separately printed I have been favoured with various criticisms. One is of such importance that I cannot reprint them without taking note of it. Mr. David Eichholz of Bristol University points out to me that, although the opinion has been widespread that Aristotle did not write what has come down to us as the Fourth Book of his *Meteorology*, in fact in two passages of his writings (*Parts of Animals* 649a and *Generation of Animals* 784b) he accepts conclusions established in this book as the considered statement of his own views. The inference seems certain that *Meteorology* IV is a genuine work of Aristotle. This conclusion affects two passages in my book. (1) On pages 23 and 24 the praise I accord to *Meteorology* IV should go to Aristotle, not to pseudo-Aristotle. (2) On pages 51–53 our complaint should be, not that Aristotle never tried by experiment to ascertain the properties of materials, but that later generations neglected his experiments and honoured his *a priori* theorizings.

I
THE CHARACTER OF EARLY GREEK SCIENCE

IN the opening chapters of his *Metaphysics* Aristotle seeks to define that First Philosophy or Theology which is the subject of his work. He describes the stages of intellectual development through which mankind has passed. He tells us that in man *memory* gives rise to *experience* and that experience in turn gives rise to *science* and *art*. The gradual perfection of the arts provides man with the necessities of life and with the social refinements. Then, "when everything of this kind has already been provided," there emerge sciences which deal neither with the necessities nor the refinements of life. These deal with first causes and principles and are properly called *wisdom*. Wisdom of this sort is the subject-matter of the inquiry pursued throughout the many books of the *Metaphysics*.

Aristotle sought the beginning of this wisdom in the early Milesian philosophers. He regarded the philosophy expounded in his *Metaphysics* as the culmination of a movement of thought begun by them. He tells us that the early philosophers each put forward a single material substance as the First Principle of all that exists. According to him, their systems of thought all conform to the type known as material monism. Aristotle completes the structure of their thought by adding to the material cause of existence three immaterial types of cause—efficient, final, and formal. This cannot be accepted as a completely true account of early Greek thought. Milesian philosophy did not emerge *after* the necessities and refinements of life had been provided for. It arose in the course of a great wave of economic and political progress, and its essential character, as I shall argue, was that it applied ideas derived from techniques of production to the interpretation of the phenomena of the universe. The metaphysical thought of Aristotle did not continue this mode of philosophizing.

That Aristotle himself was not unaware of a certain difficulty in attaching his metaphysical speculations to the active and operational philosophy of the Milesians appears plainly in what he says. He insists that what he calls wisdom is not a *productive* science. " That it is not a productive science," he adds, " is clear *even* from consideration of the earliest philosophies." That little word " even " speaks volumes. As we shall see before we are done, its meaning is " in spite of all appearances to the contrary." In fact the fragments of the old philosophers are full of allusions to the productive arts. It is these allusions that we shall principally be concerned to examine. We shall find, I think, that it was precisely because these arts were productive that they seemed to the first philosophers to constitute true knowledge of the nature of things.

A distinguished French historian of culture, Felix Sartiaux, regards the metaphysics of the Greeks as not essentially different from the thought of other ancient peoples, and as not constituting, therefore, the chief claim of the Greeks to originality. There is, he suggests, a striking similarity between Hindu philosophy and Platonic idealism. But Greek science is unique. In Sartiaux's phrase, it constitutes a *mutation* in human thinking.[1] This is a happier metaphor than some that have been employed in this connection. The question I am seeking to answer in this essay is, In what precisely did this mutation consist ?

It has been usual to define the new attitude of the Milesian thinkers by saying that they were the first to attempt a purely rational explanation of the universe. This seems plainly incorrect. The first assertion of reason as the sole guide to the nature of Being was made by Parmenides in opposition to the older mode of research by eye, ear, and tongue, that is, by the senses of sight, hearing, and taste.[2] This rational method has been made familiar to us by Plato in many of his dialogues. The earlier thinkers offered an explanation of the universe in terms of familiar operations by which they exercised control over limited portions of it. They might be said to have given an operational rather than a rational account of the nature of things. Their criterion of truth was successful practice. The exaltation by them of the practical knowledge contained in the techniques into a method of analysis of natural phenomena was the truly revolutionary step.

In Egypt and Babylon the control over nature exercised in the techniques threw little light on the processes of nature as a whole. Practice did not pass beyond the domain of practice. The domain of nature was already occupied by mythology. Mythology and technology constituted two entirely different fields of knowledge. With the Milesians technology drove mythology off the field. The central illumination of the Milesians was the notion that the whole universe works in the same way as the little bits of it that are under man's control. The vast phenomena of nature, so awe-inspiring in their regularity or their capriciousness, in their beneficence or their destructiveness, had been the domain of myth. Now they were seen to be not essentially different from the familiar processes engaged in by the cook, the farmer, the potter, and the smith. This involved on the one hand a hardy assault on the divine majesty of celestial phenomena, and on the other it meant a sudden exaltation of the intelligence and power of man. Every human technique acquired a double character. It remained an approved traditional method of achieving a limited practical end. It became a revelation of the true nature of cosmic phenomena. The processes men controlled on earth became the key to the whole activity of the universe.

It may be asked why it is not immediately obvious

from the fragments that remain that this is the character of early Greek science. The answer is that our first systematic account of the opinions of the early thinkers comes to us from the pen of a man who was interested in them primarily in so far as they could be made to illustrate his own outlook on the world. We are compelled to see the early Greek thinkers through the distorting medium of the writings of Aristotle.

Ten years ago an elaborate investigation of the kind and degree of distortion produced by this medium was carried out by an American scholar, Harold Cherniss.[3] He observes that Aristotle's belief " that all previous theories were stammering attempts to express his own aids him in interpreting those theories out of all resemblance to their original form," with the result that Aristotle " sets the history of philosophy on its head by attributing to the earliest thinkers a strictly logical conception of identity." Aristotle reduced all the Ionic theories to the formula of material monism. Cherniss finds in them no evidence of material monism at all. " Instead there appears to be a steady and swift development of the problem of change." Summing up, Cherniss concludes that " the use to which in his writings Aristotle has put the Presocratic theories has not only perverted the details but has also obliterated the problems these theories had to meet and obscured the relationship of the doctrines to one another."

If, then, we abandon the idea that the philosophy of the Milesian thinkers was material monism, what are we to substitute for this description? Cherniss claims that these early philosopher-scientists were interested in " physical processes of all kinds." He is correct in asserting that their interest was in change, but physical processes *of all kinds* is too comprehensive a phrase. One is reminded of Tolstoy's quarrel with the scientists who claimed to study *everything*. " But really *everything* is too much," protested Tolstoy. " Everything is an infinite quantity of objects. It is impossible at one and the same time to study all." We may be quite sure that the early Greek thinkers did not study physical processes of all kinds. It will be appropriate to consider what factors in the conditions of their age must have determined their interests.

We are all now adherents in some degree of the *gestalt* psychology. We realize that perception is of a whole situation, a complex of events, a "configuration," a synthesis; and that the process of understanding is a process of analysis. Science as it progresses makes for itself an equipment of concepts which are the tools by which it analyses the complex phenomena of experience. These mental tools have their history, like their material counterparts of stone and metal. Too often the modern historian of ancient thought fails to detect and describe the analytical tools of his predecessors. The result is that, without this clue, ancient science appears almost indistinguishable from the developed science of our own day. When Fisher, in his *History of Europe*, wrote: "The curiosity of the Greeks was lively and universal. No problem suggested by the contemplation of the mysterious universe was too remote, too sacred, or too abstruse, to abash their refreshing audacity," he was making too big a claim. The contemplation of the mysterious universe means different things at different times, and in the toilsome progress of science, which depends on many complicated social factors, audacity is not enough. To make my meaning clear I propose to examine a short passage of an ancient work of science in order to disclose in it not so much the opinions as the analytical tools of the writer. I shall choose a passage from the Roman poet Lucretius because we have the whole of his work and can thus be more confident in our interpretation of his meaning. But I think I shall be able to satisfy you, before I finish, that in his scientific method he was a true disciple, even too true a disciple, of those early Greeks whose opinions as modified by Epicurus form the subject-matter of his poem.

In the passage I have chosen [4] Lucretius discusses certain changes which occur in nature. I select four : (1) erosion of their banks by rivers; (2) the carrying off of the surface water from the sea by strong winds; (3) evaporation of the sea by the sun's rays; and (4) the supposed filtering of the salt out of sea-water by the action of the earth. The first process, erosion of river-banks, is described in these words: *ripas radentia flumina rodunt.* This is generally translated: rivers as they glide past gnaw their banks. This, I contend, is a mistranslation. The word *radentia* here is not a poetically descriptive epithet, but a functional one. It does not here mean to *glide past*, but to *rasp*. The sense is: rivers by rasping erode their banks. This interpretation is confirmed by the fact that *ramenta* (filings or shavings) is the Latin for alluvial gold found in rivers.[5] Secondly, we come to the action of wind on surface water. Here the Latin is: *validi verrentes aequora venti diminuunt.* This is generally translated: the winds as they sweep over the sea lessen it. But we may ask, *How* do they lessen it? Lucretius has given the answer. The *validi venti* do something appropriate to them. They *verrunt*, that is, *brush* the sea. The word does not simply express the poetical notion we convey when we speak of winds sweeping over the sea. They are not sweeping *over* the sea, they are sweeping the sea itself away. The thought is that of Francis Bacon in his charming introduction to his *Historia Ventorum*, where he says of the winds: *terrae autem (quae gentis humanae sedes est et domicilium) scopae sunt :* the earth is man's home and the winds are the brooms that clean it. What Lucretius means is: breezes are brooms which brush away the sea. When he comes to the third topic, the action of the sun on water, he uses a very striking phrase. The process of evaporation by the sun is described in these words: *radiis retexens aetherius sol.* Munro loosely translates: the sun decomposes the sea with his rays. *Retexere* means to unweave. *Radius*, in Latin, means both ray and shuttle. There is a play on words. The sun is said to unweave the water by its shuttling rays. That implies that the sea is a sort of fabric, a woven fabric, a view which is plainly stated elsewhere in the poem.[6] The epithet applied to the sun is also important. The sun is called *aetherius*, and the ether is the element that is potentially fire. Fire is the most active among the elements, and its action on the grosser and more passive elements is to unweave their fabric. Now we come to the fourth and last of the processes I have selected for examination. Some of the ancients supposed that the ocean is the source of all rivers. That presented them with several problems, among them the facts that the sea is salt and the rivers fresh. They attempted to solve that problem by saying that the earth is a kind of filter which takes the salt out of the sea.[7] This is the meaning of the Lucretian phrase: *percolatur virus*, the salt is filtered out. We have now considered Lucretius' explanation of four natural processes with a view to finding the analytical tools which he employed for their interpretation. What we have found is what we should have expected to find if we were in the habit of thinking historically. We find a collection of the simple implements with which man at that time attempted to adapt his environment to suit his needs. We find the rasp, the broom, the shuttle, and the filter.

I must not pause here to discuss the merits or defects of this method of analysis at any length. It is not an experimental method, for it is assumed that a filter could remove salt from the sea. It would appear that the poet did not distinguish between a substance in solution and a substance in suspension. It reveals, to my mind, considerable strength in the way it distinguishes between the action of wind and sun on water. By the contrast between the action of loom and broom, evaporation is shown to be a subtler thing than the bodily removal of surface water by the wind. But these details must not concern us now. Enough if we begin to grasp more clearly what went on in the head of an ancient natural philosopher when he contemplated the mysterious universe. He could not rise above the technical level of his age. He must perforce attempt to interpret changes taking place spontaneously in nature in the light of such changes as man himself was at that time capable of producing.

Before I leave Lucretius I shall take two further examples of his method of interpreting nature in the light of techniques. Everybody remembers his description of the universe as *moles et machina mundi*,[8] the massive machine of the world. What he might have in mind in using this phrase is suggested when he proceeds to offer possible explanations of the motion of the stars. He thinks they might be moving round on a great wheel blown by a stream of wind, "just as we see streams of water turning round wheels with their scoops." This example has a peculiar interest because, if our recent historians of techniques are right, the water-wheel was not in use in the Mediterranean world before about the middle of the first century B.C. This contemporary illustration could not have been borrowed by the Roman poet from his Greek sources. It represents an original application by him of a traditional method of interpretation.

My second example is of deeper import. Lucretius has a very striking epithet which he applies both to earth and nature. He speaks of *daedala tellus*, and of *natura daedala rerum*. What does this word *daedala* mean? Daedalus was the Cretan engineer who built the labyrinth, invented the saw and the compass, and made wings for his son Icarus and himself. It is clear, then, that by the choice of this word Lucretius meant to describe the earth and nature as ingenious and inventive in the highest degree. The spontaneous processes of earth and nature seem to him to embody skill and artifice. Do we not here again meet nature with her rasp, her broom, her loom, and her filter? The earth is *daedala tellus* to one who is accustomed to interpret her activities in the light of human techniques.

It is time now to turn to the fragments of the Presocratics themselves and ask how far they bear out the interpretation I have suggested. The first of the Milesian philosophers who committed anything to writing was Anaximander. He describes the world as coming into being by a process of separation of different elements out of an original indeterminate mass. First fire separated from the rest and enclosed them. Then the action of fire on the remaining mass produced a further separation. Vapour or air was sucked up and earth began to separate from water. With the continuation of this process the vapour burst the fiery envelope which enclosed the world. The vapour enfolded the torn fragments of the fiery envelope and formed tubes of mist enclosing wheels of fire, which rotated about the earth. The resulting picture was a very strange one. The earth was regarded as a shallow cylinder floating in the sea. The fiery wheels revolved about it in the plane of the ecliptic. The heavenly bodies were punctures in the tubes of mist, through which the fire rushed out. Eclipses were caused by the closing of these holes. In this picture, which is at once so grandiose and homely, interpreters have not failed to see a variety of concepts derived from techniques. The older mythologists had conceived of the sun as a wheel and imagined the sun god to be driving his chariot across the sky. They, too, had taken a suggestion from a technique, but they were specially concerned to do the sun god honour. Gods, like kings, must ride in cars. But Anaximander interpreted the sun's motion not after the action of a chariot wheel used for transport, but after the action of a wheel which revolves without changing its position; that is to say, the potter's wheel. In making this suggestion he was felt by conservative opinion not to be doing honour to the sky god, but to be abolishing him. Zeus had been dethroned and a new god, *Dinos* or Rotation, had taken his place.[9] Much uneasiness was felt at this technician's interpretation of the universe. So also those jets of fire bursting through vents, which he used to explain the stars, could have been suggested by nothing but the bellows in the blast furnace. Equally clearly the plane in which the fiery wheels revolved implies acquaintance with the *polos*, that is to say the hemispherical concave sun-dial which had been introduced from Mesopotamia. We have already found the thought of Lucretius guided in his interpretation of nature by the rasp, the broom, the shuttle, and the filter. I said then that we should have evidence that this was the method of the first Greek scientists. Now we find the thought of the first Greek to write a book *On Nature* guided by the potter's wheel, the sun-dial, and the bellows.

The successor of Anaximander, Anaximenes, made two great advances by the same method. He gave a much more consistent account than his master of the process by which one form of matter might be changed into another. Anaximander had bequeathed him a picture of the universe separated out into four elements of differing densities: Fire, Mist, Water, and Earth. Anaximenes now advanced the idea that the qualitative differences between them might be reduced to quantitative ones. He thought that Fire, by being more closely packed, turned into Mist; Mist into Water; Water into Earth. Whence did he derive this idea? I think I am right in saying that all commentators are now agreed, from the evidence of his vocabulary, that his idea was derived from the process of felting as practised in his native town of Miletus, which was famous for its woollen manufacture. In felting, the loose woven fabrics are subjected to heat and pressure and emerge reduced in volume but increased in density. The fulling-mill was thus the source of this brilliant suggestion. A second great advance on his master also stands to the credit of Anaximenes. Anaximander had ranged the elements in the order of their density from Earth at the centre to Fire at the outside. The heavenly bodies were conceived of as made purely of Fire. We find that his pupil Anaximenes, however, doubtless in the effort to account for the fall of meteoric substances from the sky, is willing to put earth and stones in the heavens. He feels justified in doing this on the evidence of the sling. This, being attached to the human hand, reveals even better than the potter's wheel the nature of centrifugal force. After Anaximenes it was legitimate to regard the heavenly bodies as lumps of earth. This was an achievement of what I call the operational interpretation of nature. Plato, who was a rationalist in the tradition of Parmenides, struggled from first to last—that is to say, from the *Apology* to the *Laws*—to get the earth and stones out of the sky again.[10] Aristotle, at the time when he followed in the same tradition, completed the work of Plato by making the heavenly bodies of a special celestial substance. But these ideas came later. The chief clue to the world-picture of the Milesian philosophers is to be derived from the potter's wheel, the bellows, the fulling-mill, and the sling.

I cannot now pursue this line of inquiry through the fragments of the rest of the Presocratics. For this I shall refer to a brief, balanced, and brilliant statement by the veteran historian Rudolfo Mondolfo, which has recently been published.[11]

We must now turn to consider how this mode of inquiry developed into a technique of experiment, so far as it can be said to have done so. What we have got so far is a very different thing from mere observation of uncontrolled natural phenomena, but it does not amount to systematic experimentation. Rather, suggestions derived from technical processes are applied very boldly, but also very vaguely, to the interpretation of the major phenomena of nature. One of the first definite indications of a narrower and more precisely determined application of this method occurs in the middle of the fifth century. Here we get something that might be called a crucial experiment.

The Sicilian philosopher Empedocles suspected a connection between the supposed tidal movement of the blood in the human body and the pressure of the outside air. Before his time the nature of the still, invisible air as a resistant medium was not clearly understood. Men understood that wind could exercise pressure, but they did not know that wind was simply air in motion. Empedocles, as everybody knows, made use of the pipette, or toddy-lifter, to perform a simple series of experiments which anybody could repeat. These conclusively demonstrated that the invisible motionless air is a resistant medium. This demonstration of Empedocles had been preceded by the Pythagorean demonstration of the relation of the pitch of a note to the length of the vibrating medium. It was accompanied by an explicit defence of the use of sense evidence against the attack on its use by Parmenides.[12] By the middle of the fifth century some scientists had taken the step forward to true experimentation. But this is an exceedingly difficult step and established itself very slowly. The older method of relying on rather vague suggestions from techniques generally persisted. Crucial experiments are not easy to devise.

The consequences of Empedocles' demonstration of the corporeal nature of the invisible and motionless air were felt all over the field of Greek science. I have time now to mention only one of them which, so far as I know, has escaped notice. The Greeks must often have speculated about the flight of birds. It must have been obvious that birds could sail. The human technique of *sailing* would throw light on this function of the wing of a bird. But how did birds propel themselves through the sky on a windless day? Nobody could say, and nobody did say, until Empedocles had shown that the air was a resistant medium. Then the solution followed quickly. It is given in the opening chorus of the *Agamemnon* of Aeschylus, who was well acquainted with Sicily and must certainly have known the work of its philosopher-poet. Aeschylus compares the two sons of Atreus starting off in their ships for Troy, to two eagles wheeling about their plundered nest. The eagles, like the ships, are said to be *rowing*—πτερύγων ἐρετμοῖσιν ἐρεσσόμενοι—" with a wheel and whirr as of winged oars beating the waves of the wind," as Professor Thomson renders it. Once it was clear that the air was a resistant medium like the sea, the human technique of rowing was available to explain the natural phenomenon of flying. Aeschylus seems to be the first to express this idea. In the *Odyssey* (bk. 11, 125) oars are called the wings of ships, but this is not the same as calling wings the oars of birds. It does not give a clear answer to the problem of flight.

It is an interesting confirmation of this interpretation of the passage of Aeschylus to turn to the first mention in Latin literature of the mechanics of flight. It occurs in the *Annales* of the old Roman poet Ennius, in a passage which appears unaccountably laboured until we understand the difficulties with which the poet was contending.[13] The Latin language had no word of its own by which to distinguish air from wind, but Ennius, who knew all about Empedocles, was determined to make his barbarous Roman audience understand how a bird flies. He, too, like Aeschylus, had occasion to mention the flight of the eagle, but he could not, like Aeschylus, say bluntly that it was rowing. What he does say is this: An eagle was flying supporting itself by its closely-set feathers on the wind, which the Greeks in their language call air. In other words, there was no wind, but only air, to express which idea Ennius had to call in the aid of Greek. With later Latin poets the phrase *remigium alarum*, the oarage of the wings, became a commonplace. Attention to the passages in which it occurs will reveal that it is generally the mechanics of flight, not a picturesque comparison with a trireme, that is in the poet's mind (*e.g.*, Ovid, *Metamorphoses*, viii, 228).

The poets reveal to us how the human techniques

of sailing and rowing may be applied to the elucidation of the flight of birds. Let us now cite an example of this scientific method from a very different sphere. At the end of the fifth century B.C. a Greek physician, whose work shows proof of acquaintance with the systems of Heraclitus, Empedocles, and Anaxagoras, thought of interpreting human physiology in this way.[14] His problem is to find a method of bringing physiological processes under observation. This, he says, cannot be done directly, but there is fortunately a domain in which man has brought processes under intelligent control—namely, the techniques. We must, then, says our physician, make use of the techniques to throw light on the hidden physiology of man. This we can do, he proceeds—and this is the heart of his thought—because technical processes are really copies or imitations of natural processes. Here is a close translation of the words in which he describes his proposed method: " Men do not understand how to observe the invisible by means of the visible. Their techniques resemble the physiological processes of man, but men do not know this. But the fact is that the mind of the gods has taught men to imitate their bodily functions in their techniques. But though men understand the technical processes, they fail to understand the natural processes imitated by the techniques." Our physician then proceeds to list the techniques which he thinks are imitated from processes in the human body and the study of which can throw light on human physiology. The techniques he mentions are those of the smith, the fuller, the cobbler, the carpenter, the builder, the musician, the currier, the basket-maker, the gold-refiner, the statuary, the potter, and the scribe. He does not succeed in isolating any single problem susceptible of being solved by a crucial experiment, as Empedocles did; but he does show us a determined and systematic attempt to go forward on the path marked out nearly two hundred years earlier by the Milesian philosophers.

I have now described what I conceive to have been the essential character of the mutation in thought which we associate with the Milesian philosophers of the first half of the sixth century. It remains to consider the historical conditions under which this movement in thought occurred. Do we know anything about Miletus, about Ionia, about the character of the people and their civilization, which makes it natural to connect this occurrence with this time and place?

In the old bronze-age civilizations of the valleys of the Nile and the Euphrates there was a high degree of technical development. But the ideas derived from the techniques could not be applied to the interpretation of the major phenomena of nature because the domain of nature was already occupied by an elaborate mythology handed down by priestly corporations. This mythology is incorrectly described as popular superstition. It was the official view of the nature of the universe which it would be impious to question because it was enforced by authority. There were various kinds of knowledge in these old bronze-age civilizations. There was, on the one hand, the practical knowledge necessary for the control of nature by such techniques as those of the farmer, the potter, and the smith. This was passed on orally to apprentices. There were certain techniques, like the control of the water-supply, the redivision of lands, and the erection of great buildings, which were in the hands of the ruling and literate class and gave birth to sciences which were emerging from the purely practical stage—sciences such as positional astronomy and mensuration. Over and above these there was a vast mass of myth and legend, constituting an anonymous, incoherent literature clumsily expressed in hieratic language, which accounted for the major phenomena of nature and was maintained by the rulers as a necessary basis of the social order. What we call science, in modern times, could not begin to emerge until the barriers between these different spheres of knowledge were broken down, until the suggestions derived from technical processes could be boldly applied to the whole domain of nature, until the spell of the mythological mode of explanation was broken, and until the emerging mathematical disciplines ceased to be part of the administrative equipment of bureaucrats and became part of the culture of the free citizen. It was in Ionia that the social conditions requisite for this advance first appeared.

In the third millennium B.C. Asia Minor revolved in the orbit of the civilizations of Mesopotamia and Egypt. In the second millennium it began to make decisive contributions of its own to the sum of world civilization. Among these was the working of iron. This brought about a radical change in the basis of society.[15] Iron is much more abundant than copper, and can be mined more easily. In the bronze-age civilizations the trade in copper was in the hands of the small ruling class, which gathered the tiny surplus of food from hundreds of thousands of serfs, traded it for copper and tin, and distributed the raw materials to the artisans in the workshops of the king or the nobles. When the secret of iron-smelting began to spread abroad, any village could equip itself with agricultural implements or weapons of war. Civilizations of a different type, more democratically based than those of the bronze-age States, began to assert their independence of the older centres of power. In Asia Minor new peoples appear on the stage of history. First the Hittites, then the Phrygians, the Lydians, and others create new forms of society. Asia Minor, and especially its western seaboard, becomes the home of an indigenous culture.

A similar movement was taking place on the mainland of Greece. There the outposts of the bronze-age civilization of Crete, at such centres as Tiryns, Argos, and Mycenae, went down before the northern immigrants with their iron-age technique. These new-comers, who had been lifted out of the tribal stage by the spread of iron-age culture, still preserved much of the outlook characteristic of tribal society. This they brought with them when, in the second half of the second millennium, they overflowed the boundaries of Greece proper and began to win for themselves a new home on the Aegean coast of Anatolia. These Greek settlers had already, in mainland Greece, been in contact with the Mycenean culture which had spread from Crete. In their new home they found new educators—the Phrygians, the Lydians, the Lycians, the Carians. They were, in fact, settling not only in one of the most favoured spots climatically speaking, but also at the cross-roads of all the civilizations of the ancient world.

For those historians who like to ascribe the achievements of the Ionians to their being Greeks, it is unfortunate to have to face the fact that they were of mixed racial composition. The settlers freely intermarried with the Asiatic peoples. This notably differentiated them from the Greeks of the homeland. Euripides describes the coast of Anatolia as the land " whose fair-walled towns hold a mixed population of Greeks and barbarians." [16] Whether or not this cross-breeding was of advantage to them, they had every cultural stimulus to originality and inventiveness. They were immigrants from the mainland of Greece who had left their native soil because, as younger sons or the sons of concubines, they were crowded off the land which had passed out of tribal into individual ownership. As Burnet has remarked, they were a people without a past. True, strong traces of their tribal outlook survive in their philosophy. These have been explored by various writers. The late Professor Cornford, in an early work, *From Religion to Philosophy*, reminds us that the key-words of Greek philosophy trail after them meanings derived from their origin in tribal society. Professor George Thomson, in his *Aeschylus and Athens*, has greatly deepened and enriched our understanding of this debt. Hans Kelsen, in his very recent study, *Society and Nature*, has shown independently that with primitive peoples the social law of retribution, the *lex talionis*, covers all the phenomena of nature, and how slowly, even among the Greeks, this idea gave place to recognition of the distinction between society and nature. But once tribal society had been superseded, tribal ideas also began to give way. The principal agent in the break up of tribal society was the development of productive techniques. The same agent which broke up tribal society also broke up tribal mentality. It was the techniques that first made clear to man that nature was governed by laws of a character essentially different from the law of retribution.[17]

There was another cultural advantage enjoyed by the Asiatic Greeks the importance of which it would be difficult to over-estimate. The Greek alphabet came into existence among them, probably in the ninth century, owing to their close contact and keen rivalry with the Phoenicians, from whom they borrowed the idea of a phonetic script. "The invention of more precise, simple and easily formed signs than those of the earlier writings . . . exercised a decisive effect on the development of civilization by putting within the reach of all a practice which up till then had been the preserve of a privileged caste of clerks and scribes." This was an invention as important for the rise of democracy as the smelting of iron. The smelting of iron and the phonetic alphabet do not explain Greek civilization. What historical event is ever completely explicable? The process of history is a creative process. New things are always coming out of the womb of time. But it is reasonable to assert that Greek civilization is not conceivable before the smelting of iron and the invention of the alphabet. These inventions, with all that they implied, formed the basis of the new type of city created by these Asiatic Greeks. Now, for the first time, we find the city-state, a community in which laws are understood to be public enactments made for the common good. This was a new thing. It was part of the

THE CHARACTER OF EARLY GREEK SCIENCE 19

mental background of the first philosophers. "The people must fight for their laws as they would for their walls," said Heraclitus.

It was from Attica, Phocis, and the Peloponnesus that the Greek immigrants came who settled in Ionia. Seizing the coastal islands first, they next got a footing on the promontories and the deep gulfs of that heavily indented coastline. Soon they spread over the rich valleys of the Hermus, Cayster, and Maeander. Eventually there came to be a dozen famous towns grouped in a loose confederation, maintaining themselves in a considerable degree of political independence of the not very aggressive Lydian kings, with their capital at Sardis. Chios, Samos, Teos, Lebedos, Ephesus, Miletus, Clazomenae, Phocaea, Erythrae, Colophon, Myus, and later Smyrna—these were the towns of the Ionian confederation in which the characteristic civilization of the Greek peoples first took shape. So mightily did they prosper that Ionia in its turn overflowed and became the centre of one of the most important colonizing movements in all history. By the sixth century their colonies were scattered all over the Mediterranean coast, from the innermost recesses of the Black Sea to distant Spain. Miletus alone was the mother-city of eighty daughter-States.[18]

It was out of this immensely active, constructive, and progressive civilization that Greek science sprang. If there is one thing that characterizes this age more than another, it is that at this period the great thinkers were also men of action. It was an age when the highest honours were gladly accorded to the technician. Not all traditional ascriptions of inventions to their authors are reliable but no other age in Greek history can supply such a list of men honoured for their practical achievements as this. It is quite typical of the age that Anacharsis the Scythian, who was the contemporary of Thales and Anaximander, was renowned for his invention or improvement of the anchor, the bellows, and the potter's wheel. Shortly after his date Glaucus of Chios invented the technique of soldering iron. About the middle of the sixth century Chersiphron of Cnossus and his son, Metagenes, built the temple of Artemis at Ephesus and won renown for the transport and erection of the columns and architraves. Herodotus devotes exceptional attention to the affairs of the Samians on the ground that their island was the scene of three of the greatest achievements of the Greek people. They are all feats of engineering—the tunnelling of the hill of Castro by Eupalinus of Megara, the construction of a great mole in the sea to protect the harbour, and the building of the greatest temple Herodotus had ever seen by the local architect Rhoecus.[19] The son of Rhoecus, Theodorus of Samos, was one of the greatest engineers and inventors of all time. He is credited with the introduction of many novelties—the level, the square, the rule, the lathe,[20] the key; a method of polishing the surface of precious stones; a technique of solidifying marshy ground to receive the foundations of great buildings. Above all, to him belongs the chief credit for the invention and perfection of the technique of bronze-casting. On this Casson remarks that it involved "a logically developed series of inventions which all culminated in the final intricate and elaborate process which in substance has remained unaltered and incapable of alteration down to to-day. . . . Only a people accustomed to use their hands and wits in perfect combination could so early have mastered so complicated a process."[21] It would be easy to extend this list of great engineers, metallurgists, and inventors. But enough has been said to illustrate the character of the time. Enough, too, perhaps has been said to suggest that, if early Greek philosophy was interested in the process of change, it was not simply because nature is so changeable (that had always been true), but because man himself had never before been so active and independent an agent of change. The men who built the cities of Ionia were a new type of men, who had effected an "outstanding enlargement in man's control over nature." [22]

Now it needs no elaborate argument to prove that our Milesian philosophers were typical men of their age. Thales was a famous man for more than two centuries before Aristotle brought him on the scene as the first metaphysician; but he does not appear in that character before Aristotle. For Herodotus he is the engineer who was said to have turned the course of the River Halys for Croesus; or the astronomer who foretold the year of an eclipse of the sun; or the wise political adviser of the Ionian confederation who urged them to create a common capital at Teos. Others describe him as the introducer of an improved technique of navigation derived like the alphabet from the Phoenicians. Even for Plato [23] he is still the ingenious inventor to be mentioned in the same breath with Anarcharsis, by reason of his practical achievements. Anaximander, the second of the Milesians, was not only the first to write a book *On Nature*, but he was also the first to construct a map and the leader of one of the expeditions to found a distant colony. A century later, Miletus was still producing the same type of man—the philosopher who is also a man of action. Hippodamus, the greatest town-planner of antiquity, might be described as a Pythagorean engineer. His philosophy was the source of his innovations in town-planning.

"The ancients," says Francis Bacon, "wrote much natural history, but neglected the inquiry into the mechanical arts. Yet it is the mechanical arts which give the better insight into the secret places of nature. Uncontrolled nature, with her profusion and spontaneity, dissipates the powers of the understanding, and by her variety confounds them. In mechanical operations the attention is concentrated, and the modes and processes of nature, not merely her effects, are seen." In making these animadversions on the natural history of the Greeks, Bacon expressly confined himself to the post-Platonic schools. He was aware that the Presocratics should be exempted from their application. Of the earlier systems he says: " They have got something of natural philosophy in them, they smack of the nature of things, of experience and of bodies." [24] And this, of course, was because the minds of these early thinkers were not dissipated by observation of uncontrolled nature, but guided and controlled by attention to the mechanical arts.

Elsewhere Bacon defines the kind of natural history at which he aims: " We seek a history not only of nature as she exists free and unconfined, when she flows along spontaneously accomplishing her tasks. Such is the history of the heavens, of meteorology, of earth and sea, of minerals, of plants, of animals. But much more we seek the history of nature constrained and vexed, that is to say of nature thrust from her original state mastered and modified by the art and agency of man." [25] These are words of wisdom. The distinction between *natura libera* and *natura vexata* lies at the basis of science. It was the Ionian Greeks, boldly planning to master and modify nature by the art and agency of man, who first drew a firm distinction between nature and society, between the environment man shares with the animals and what he has made out of it for himself. Only when this distinction had been clearly drawn, when the unique position of man in the universe had been clearly realized, was it possible for the philosopher to ask himself what is the relation between humanly controlled processes and natural processes. This was the root of our science.

Elsewhere again Bacon writes: " Prejudice has stood in the way of research into nature through the avenue of the mechanical arts, but we must lay aside such pride. Among the arts we must prefer those which reveal the natural bodies and materials of things by changing and adapting them. Such arts are agriculture, cooking, chemistry, dyeing, glass-making, enamelling, sugar-making, powder-making, fire-works,

THE CHARACTER OF EARLY GREEK SCIENCE 23

paper-making and so on." [26] Historically, we know that this prejudice increased among the Greeks with the growth of slavery. In so far as they succumbed to the prejudices it engendered, they cut themselves off from the tap-root from which the sap of science is drawn. Severed from its tap-root, Greek science grew into a sickly plant in which the logical element remained strong but the factual element dwindled. But so long as it remained active, it could not dispense with the evidence of the arts by which man vexes nature.

It may be well to cite further examples of Greek works of science in which this method is employed. The most impressive fifth-century scientific work extant in its entirety is the Hippocratic tract called *On Ancient Medicine*. It is the work of a dietician or cook who systematically exploits the evidence derived from his profession to reveal to him the nature of health and disease. About a hundred years later the pseudo-Aristotelian treatise *On Colours* reveals everywhere the debt of the author to the dyeing industry. Still more remarkable is another pseudo-Aristotelian writing, *Meteorology* IV, a document of first importance for the history of Greek science. Early in this work there is a comparison of the natural processes of ripening and digestion with the technical processes of cooking. Broiling and boiling, we are told, are both technical and natural processes. It makes no difference whether the processes take place " in kitchen utensils or in the organs of plants and animals," for " techniques are a copy of nature." Finally, after discussing a very wide range of technical processes of which the most interesting perhaps are pottery and metallurgy, the author launches into a fascinating attempt to classify things in accordance with their aptitude to react to human violence. " Let us begin," he writes, " by enumerating those qualities expressing the aptitude or inaptitude of a thing to be affected in a certain way. They are as follows: to be apt or inapt to solidify, melt, be softened by heat, be softened by water, bend, break, be comminuted, impressed, moulded, squeezed; to be tractile or non-tractile, malleable or non-malleable, to be fissile or non-fissile, apt or inapt to be cut; to be viscous or friable, compressible or incompressible, combustible or incombustible; to be apt or inapt to give off fumes." Here is a real Baconian programme of research dating from about the turn of the fourth into the third century B.C. Though almost certainly not the work of Aristotle, it belongs to the Peripatetic school and marks a stage in the recovery of that school from the dominance of abstract mathematics which characterized the Academy.

It is an error on the part of some modern historians of science, when they discuss the opinions of the Greeks on the criterion of truth, to represent the schools as divided in their allegiance between the evidence of the senses and the deductions of reason. The conflict lies deeper than a dispute between reason and the senses. I may be allowed again to appeal to Francis Bacon. He saw clearly that the advance of knowledge depends neither on the unaided senses nor the unaided reason, but on practice. He characterized it as "a grave error to regard sense as the measure of things," urging instead that "the delicacy of experiments is far beyond that of the senses, even when assisted by the choicest instruments. Accordingly," says he, "I do not attach much importance to direct sense-perception in itself; my method is to let the senses judge the experiment but to let the experiment judge the fact." It was practice, too, not mere observation, that lay at the base of Greek science. In the earliest period the practice might be described as industrial rather than experimental, but it slowly developed into an experimental technique.

It is time now to bring this essay to an end, and I shall do so with a description of the character and content of Presocratic science from the pen of no less a man than Plato himself. The passage, which occurs in the tenth book of the *Laws*,[27] puts succinctly and brilliantly the main features of the older scientific tradition with a view to disposing of it once and for all. The passage is in the form of a dialogue between an unnamed Athenian and a Cretan called Cleinias. "According to some philosophers," says the Athenian, "the greatest and most beautiful of existing things appear to be the products of nature and of chance. Only the smaller things are products of design. Design, taking over the work by which nature brought into being those great things, forms and fashions all the smaller things, which we call products of art." Here the Cretan interrupts with a complaint that he cannot follow and the Athenian promises to be more explicit. " The elements of Fire and Water and Earth and Air, according to these philosophers, have come into existence by nature and chance and not by design. Then the bodies that come next after them, the earth, the sun, the moon, the stars, are made by these absolutely lifeless elements, when, in the course of their random combinations, they fall into appropriate relations. In this way and in no other the heavens and all that are in them have been made, and all animals and plants and all the seasons—not, mark you, by mind nor by any god nor by design but, to repeat, by nature and chance. Design or art, they say, is a later birth, a mortal thing which out of mortal elements creates certain trifles which have no great share of truth, like painting, music, and the kindred arts. *But those of the arts that do produce something serious are all those that blend their power with that of nature, like medicine, agriculture, and gymnastics.*"

Here we have, clearly expressed, the basic ideas I have been trying to put before you. Nature is blind and purposeless until the advent of man. Her reign is a reign of chance or of necessity, which are only two different aspects of the same thing. Design or purpose enters nature only with the coming of man. Human design, human technique, creates a new world, the distinctively human world. Man himself is a product of nature and can only advance by imitating nature. He constitutes the point at which nature achieves self-consciousness. But man's imitation of nature is on two levels. He has arts which merely imitate nature without altering it, like painting. These arts contain only a shadow of the truth. But in the productive arts man does not so much copy nature as co-operate with it. In Plato's phrase " he blends the power of his art with that of nature." Such arts contain truth, because, being a means of co-operation with the power of nature, successful achievement of the intended purpose means that the powers of nature have been understood. In this sense technique has both a practical and an epistemological value. Successful practice is a revelation both of man's knowledge of nature and his power over it, which are but two aspects of the one thing. Such was the idea which gripped the minds of the Milesian thinkers. It appeared then for the first time in history because then for the first time political power was in the hands of free men who were also masters of productive techniques, and who achieved an " astounding enlargement in man's control over nature." It was man's first realization that the creation of his civilization rests in his own hands, his first acceptance of this tremendous responsibility. " Where the love of mankind is there is the love of technique."[28]

References

[1] F. Sartiaux, *Histoire des religions et genèse de la métaphysique.* Bulletin de la Société Ernest Renan, No. 8, Paris, 1923. And *Les Civilisations Anciennes de l'Asie Mineure,* Paris, 1928, p. 47.

[2] Diels, *Fragmente der Vorsokratiker* (5th ed.), I, p. 234. Parmenides is attacking a method of research, not a weakness of the average man.

[3] *Aristotle's Criticism of Presocratic Philosophy.* Baltimore, 1935.

[4] V, 247–72.

[5] Pliny, *N.H.,* xxxiii, 4 (21), 66.

[6] V, 93 and 94.

THE CHARACTER OF EARLY GREEK SCIENCE 27

[7] Aristotle, *Meteorologica*, II, 2.
[8] V, 96.
[9] Aristophanes, *Clouds*, 380. The whole play is a protest, not against rationalism, but against interpreting celestial phenomena in the light of humble techniques.
[10] *Apology*, 26 C and D; *Laws*, 967 B and C.
[11] *Sugestiones de la Tecnica en las Concepciones de los Naturalistas Presocraticos*. Archeion, Nueva Serie T. 11, vol. xxiii, N. 1.
[12] Fragment 3 in Diels.
[13] et densis aquila pennis obnixa volabat vento quem perhibent Graium genus aera lingua.
[14] *Regimen*, I, xi–xxiv.
[15] See two recent books by Gordon Childe: *Progress and Archæology*, Watts (Thinker's Library), especially chap. III; and *The Story of Tools*, Cobbett Pub. Co.
[16] *Bacchae*, 17–19. See also Hippocrates, *Airs Waters Places*, xvii.
[17] See a fine passage in Sartiaux's *Morale Kantienne et Morale humaine*, p. 254, which concludes: " L'existence de la technique, qui remonte jusqu'à l'âge paléolithique, montre qu'il existe dans la pensée la plus primitive des traces d'esprit scientifique."
[18] There is a brilliant account of the development of Ionian culture in Sartiaux's book on Asia Minor already referred to.
[19] Herodotus, III, 60.
[20] If this is what τόρνος means. It is anything but certain that the Greeks knew the lathe.
[21] S. Casson, *The Technique of Early Greek Sculpture*, chap. vii.
[22] Childe, *Progress and Archæology*, p. 40.
[23] *Republic*, 600a.
[24] *Novum Organum*, I, lxiii.
[25] *Distributio Operis*.
[26] *Parasceve*, v.
[27] *Laws*, 889, slightly condensed.
[28] *Precepts*, vi., ἢν γὰρ παρῇ φιλανθρωπίη, πάρεστι καὶ φιλοτεχνίη. In the context the reference is to medicine, but the saying obviously has a wider connotation.

II

THE HAND IN HEALING: A STUDY IN GREEK MEDICINE FROM HIPPOCRATES TO RAMAZZINI

My purpose in this essay is not to discuss the details of Greek surgical practice, a subject with which I am not competent to deal. I wish rather to speak of Greek medicine as a whole and to examine the effect upon it of the Greek prejudice against manual labour. It would still more accurately define my purpose if I spoke not simply of the prejudice against manual labour, but of the decline in social status of the manual labourer which accompanied the growth of civilization. My subject lies, therefore, not within the domain of pure science, but within that of the social relations of science, and may accordingly claim to be topical.

In his treatise called *Oeconomicus*, Xenophon represents Socrates as delivering the following judgment on manual work and the manual worker. How this opinion is to be reconciled with the tradition that Socrates was himself a stonemason I cannot now pause to inquire. The question *Who was Socrates?* has hardly yet been satisfactorily answered. " What are called the mechanical arts," says Socrates, " carry a social stigma and are rightly dishonoured in our cities. For these arts damage the bodies of those who work at them or who have charge of them, by compelling the workers to a sedentary life and to an indoor life, by compelling them, indeed, in some cases to spend the whole day by the fire. This physical degeneration results also in deterioration of the soul. Furthermore, the workers at these trades simply have not got the time to perform the offices of friendship or of citizenship. Consequently they are looked upon as bad friends and bad patriots. And in some cities, especially the warlike ones, it is not legal for a citizen to ply a mechanical trade." [1]

Obviously a social division so deep as this, a cleavage which, when complete, made it impossible for the same man to be both worker and citizen, could not be without effect on the science and practice of medicine, which touch the life of every man. But the nature of this effect has, so far as my knowledge goes, been very inadequately explored.

Three topics suggest themselves to me as most likely to reveal the nature of the influence exercised on the science and art of healing by the structure of ancient classical society. First I wish to say a word about the science of anatomy and the practice of surgery. The word "surgery" is, of course, simply the modern form of the Greek *cheirourgia*, which means manual operation. And we shall find reason for connecting the decline of anatomy after Galen with the ancient prejudice against the *cheirourgos*, the surgeon or manual operator. This effect, however, was late in showing itself. It did not become fully operative until after the fall of the Western Empire.

Secondly, I wish to discuss the limitations of ancient medical science and practice in respect of the type of the person and the type of disease it habitually dealt with and habitually neglected. Roughly speaking, the working man was neglected in ancient medical practice, and the occupational disease ignored in medical science. This phenomenon is more important than the decline of anatomy and has been less noticed. It began to operate at a much earlier date, was more far-reaching in its effect, and has proved more difficult to overcome. The U.S.S.R. is the only country so far that has solved the problem of providing adequate medical attention for the whole of its working population. And it is said that the Moscow Hospital for Industrial Diseases is the only institution of its kind.

Thirdly, I shall consider a phenomenon contemporary with the dawn of Greek medical writing, though not with the dawn of Greek medicine. I mean the invasion of medical science by *a priori* philosophical concepts. In my view this is very germane to the subject of the hand in healing, for these *a priori* speculations emanated from medical amateurs who had continued to use their heads but had given up using their hands. The empty hypotheses, which began to threaten the science of medicine from the fifth century B.C. onwards, represented primarily not an aberration of the individual mind, but the emergence of a new class in society, the leisured class. For them theory bore no relation to practice. The head was independent of the hand. They were what Professor Gordon Childe has called " theoretical researchers." [2] So far as they succeeded they transformed medicine from a positive science into a speculative philosophy.

Among ancient writings, I shall be concerned chiefly with two or three treatises of the Hippocratic Corpus—*Ancient Medicine, Airs Waters Places, Regimen I–IV*. My approach to these writings is influenced chiefly by Vesalius and Ramazzini, whose able pens did full justice to the boldness and originality of their thoughts. As is but natural, their writings contain much illuminating comment on their Greek forerunners. A man who marks a turning-point in any branch of knowledge is in a very favourable position to throw light on its past. Having struggled to find the way forward, he is peculiarly aware of the obstacles that barred access to it. Being vividly conscious of the new thing he wants to say, he is vividly conscious of its absence from the tradition as he received it.

Before I turn to my first theme I should perhaps say that I have called my essay a study in Greek medicine because there was no distinctive or independent Roman medicine; and that I have ventured to extend the life of Greek medicine right down to

Ramazzini in the eighteenth century of our era because that great man still put forward his own innovations as additions to the body of Greek science and practice.

I now turn to my first topic, the decline of Greek anatomy.

In the body of his great work *De Fabrica Corporis Humani* Vesalius presents a more complete and accurate account of the structure of the human body than the Greeks had succeeded in doing. In the *Preface* he attempts to explain why the study of anatomy, which had flourished among the Greeks for so many hundreds of years, had declined after Galen. The argument advanced in this *Preface* will be our first concern.[3]

According to Vesalius, the Greek physicians, whatever sect they belonged to, the Dogmatic, Empirical, or Methodical, all agreed in employing a threefold aid to health: diet, drugs, and manual operation. " And rare indeed," he adds, " is the disease that does not require the triple treatment. A suitable diet must be prescribed, some service must be rendered by drugs and some by the hand." Nor, indeed, is the use of the hand confined to surgery. The hand also has its part to play in the preparation of food and in the compounding of drugs. Thus, if the hand is despised, every part of medicine suffers. This, according to Vesalius, is what eventually did happen.

" After the barbarian invasions," he writes, " all the sciences which before had flourished gloriously and were practised as was fitting went to ruin. At that time, and first in Italy, the more fashionable doctors, in imitation of the old Romans, began to despise the work of the hand. They delegated to slaves the manual attentions they judged needful for their patients, and themselves merely stood over them like master-builders. Then the other doctors began to follow suit. They declined the unpleasant duties of their profession without abating any of their claim to money or honour, and thus quickly fell away from the standard of the doctors of old. Methods of cooking and all the preparation of food for the sick they left to nurses; compounding of drugs they left to the apothecaries; manual operation to barbers. Thus, in course of time, the art of healing has been wretchedly rent asunder, until at last certain doctors, advertising themselves as physicians, have arrogated to themselves alone the prescription of drugs and diet for obscure diseases and have relegated the rest of medicine to those whom they call surgeons and scarcely regard as slaves, disgracefully banishing from themselves the chief and most ancient branch of the medical art and that which principally (if indeed there be any other) bases itself upon the investigation of nature."

The destructive effect on the study and teaching of anatomy of this contempt for manual operation is a commonplace. But it has never been better described than by Vesalius; and since I have been at some pains to translate it out of his elaborate Latin into simple English, I propose to quote his description here.

" When the whole conduct of manual operations," he writes, " was entrusted to barbers, not only did doctors lose the true knowledge of the viscera but the practice of dissection soon died out, doubtless for the reason that the doctors did not attempt to operate, while those to whom the manual skill was resigned were too ignorant to read the writings of the teachers of anatomy. But it is utterly impossible that this class of men should preserve for us a difficult art which they have learned only mechanically. And equally inevitably this deplorable dismemberment of the art of healing has introduced into our schools the detestable procedure now in vogue, that one man should carry out the dissection of the human body and another give the description of the parts. The latter is perched up aloft in a pulpit like a jackdaw and with a notable air of disdain he drones out information about facts which he has never approached at first hand but which he has committed to memory from the books of others, or of which he has a description before his eyes. The dissector, who is ignorant of languages, is unable to explain the dissection to the class and botches the demonstration which ought to follow the instructions of the physician, while the physician never applies his hand to the task but contemptuously steers the ship out of the manual, as the saying goes. Thus everything is wrongly taught, days are wasted in absurd questions, and in the confusion less is shown to the class than a butcher in his stall could teach a doctor."

According to Vesalius, then, the study of anatomy fell a victim to the prejudices of a slave-owning aristocracy. The period was after the fall of the Roman Empire in the West, and the blame lay principally on the Italian doctors who were corrupted by the example of the old Romans. If, as I believe, Vesalius was right in this judgment, the question at once arises why the same prejudice did not operate among the Greeks to produce the same effect.

That the Greeks early acquired a contempt for manual labour is certain. Herodotus, writing in the middle of the fifth century, already notes it. " With the Greeks," he tells us, " as with the Egyptians, Thracians, Scythians, Persians, Lydians, and almost all non-Greeks, those who learn a craft and the children of those who learn a craft are held in less esteem than the rest of the citizens. The noble are those who have escaped the yoke of manual labour. The highest honour is reserved for those who devote themselves to war." [4] This statement is in full agreement with the passage already quoted from Xenophon. The question is whether this contempt for manual labour affected the healing art among the Greeks.

At first sight it would appear certain that the general adoption of the point of view described by Herodotus and Xenophon must operate to the detriment of the science and practice of the *cheirourgos* or surgeon. In his dialogue *The Statesman*, Plato draws a distinction between a practical science like carpentry, a purely theoretical science like that of numbers, and a mixed type like architecture—in which the theoretician directs manual work in which he does not engage.[5] This is an important and necessary distinction not in itself mischievous. The mischief arose from the effort of ancient society to secure that all manual work should be done by one class, and all the thinking and directing by another. This is the vice of society on which Vesalius lays the blame for the decline of anatomy. There is a passage in Aristotle which suggests that in his day the medical art had already suffered that fatal divorce of theory from practice which Vesalius locates in Italy after the fall of the Western Empire. For Aristotle tells us that the name of physician was given to three types of men—the one who works with his hands, the one who directs the work of others, and the educated amateur.[6] Here the first would seem to represent the handicraftsman, whose social status continually declined. The second would represent the man who had shaken off the undesirable associations of a handicraft and raised himself to the status of the architect, and the third suggests the type of man who engaged only in " theoretical research."

Nevertheless I can find no clear proof that the prejudice against manual labour did, in fact, operate in Greek society to check the progress of the science of anatomy. From Alcmaeon in the fifth century B.C. to Galen in the second century A.D., the names of great anatomists are too numerous and the progress, if spasmodic, still too remarkable to warrant the assertion that the science of anatomy, before the time of Galen, suffered from the prejudice engendered by the social structure of ancient society. The careers of Aristotle, Herophilus, Erasistratus, Hegetor, Ammonius, Antyllus, Marinus, Rufus, Soranus, protest against this conclusion. Celsus, in his seventh and eighth books where he treats of surgery, lends no support to such a view. As Vesalius reminds us, Galen frequently expresses his pride in his manual skill.

We may conclude, then, that, for a reason which will be suggested at the end of this essay, the research into the structure of the human body long remained unaffected by the cause which certainly thwarted the development of other sciences among the Greeks. The cause was there but its operation was suspended. A catalytic agent was required before it could take effect, and this was not supplied until, under the Empire, the social prejudice against the slave was reinforced by the Roman prejudice against the Greek. Vesalius would appear to have defined the phenomenon with precise accuracy when he ascribed the decline of anatomy to the Italian doctors, who, in imitation of the old Romans, began to despise the work of the hand.

But when we turn to our second topic, the limitation of ancient medical practice with regard to the type of patient it habitually dealt with, the indications of the influence on medicine of the structure of society are very clear. " The sick in our cities," writes Plato in the *Laws*, " are of two classes, the slaves and the free. Slaves are for the most part attended by slaves, who run round visiting them or wait for them in their consulting rooms. There is no discussion between patient and doctor about the particulars of each case, but, with a know-all air, the doctor prescribes some rule-of-thumb remedy, like a dictator whose word must not be questioned, and skips off to attend on the next of the sick slaves, thus relieving the citizen doctor of the care of such patients. But free men are as a rule attended by a doctor who is a free man. He makes a thorough examination into the course of the disease from the beginning and into its nature, takes the patient and his friends into consultation, learns from the patient as well as teaches him, and endeavours by gentle persuasion to lead him along the path to a full recovery." [7]

The contrast here described so vividly, between the medical attention available to slaves and that available for the free, finds a parallel in the contrast between the medical requirements of the poor manual worker, who is yet a citizen, and those of the idle rich. Plato is again our informant. He is protesting against a new fashion in medicine which panders to the needs of those who have nothing to do but attend to their health. "Asclepius knew well," he makes Socrates say in *The Republic*, "that in well-ordered states every man has an occupation to which he must attend and has therefore no leisure for prolonged illnesses. The sense of this is clear to us in the case of the artisan, but, oddly enough, we do not see it in the case of the rich."

"How do you mean?" said Glaucon.

"I mean this. When a carpenter is ill he asks the physician for a rough-and-ready cure. An emetic, a purge, a cautery, or the knife—that is the remedy for him. But if some one prescribes for him a course of dietetics or tells him to wrap his head up and keep himself warm, he replies at once that he has no time to be ill, that he sees no good in a life that is spent in nursing his disease to the neglect of his customary employment. He therefore bids the doctor good-bye, resumes his ordinary way of life, and either gets well, lives, and does his business or, if his constitution fails, he dies and is rid of his troubles."

"I understand," said Glaucon, "and that, of course, is the proper use of medicine for a man in his walk of life." [8]

Familiar as these passages are, their significance was lost upon me until I read the treatise on *Occupational Diseases* of that great eighteenth-century pioneer, Bernardini Ramazzini. I call him an eighteenth-century pioneer though he was born in 1633; for he lived to be as old as Plato, dying in his eighty-first year, in 1714, and the completion of the work to which he owes his immortality belongs to the very end of his life. The full text of the *De Morbis Artificum* [9] was published only in 1713.

In the town of Modena, where Ramazzini lived, the inhabitants of the tall, crowded houses, acting up to the best sanitary standards of the time, saw to it that the cess-pits, which were connected with the drains that ran in different directions through the streets, should be cleaned out in each house once in every three years. "On one occasion," writes Ramazzini, "when that work was going forward in our house, I observed one of the labourers making extraordinary exertions to get through with his task. I pitied him on account of the cruel nature of the work and asked him why he toiled so feverishly and did not rather try to avoid exhaustion by working at a slower pace. Whereupon the poor fellow lifted his eyes up out of the pit, fixed them upon me, and said: 'No one who has not tried it can imagine what it costs to spend more than four hours in this place. It is as bad as going blind.'"

The inquiry thus auspiciously begun bore a rich fruit. Ramazzini did not forget that cleaner of privies. He was a servant of the Republic of Venice, that great city which, in his own words, "had gathered within its bosom all the arts which separately made other cities populous and rich." He was profoundly convinced of the importance of the mechanical arts for the progress of civilization. "If any one doubts their utility," he writes, "let him ponder on the difference between the Europeans and the Americans and other inhabitants of the New World." But he was equally impressed by the wretched condition of those engaged in these arts. "It must be confessed," he says, "that many arts are the cause of grave injury to those who practise them. Many an artisan has looked to his craft as a means to support life and raise a family, but all he has got from it is some deadly disease, with the result that he has departed this life cursing the craft to which he had applied himself." Ramazzini, therefore, made his resolve. "Medicine, like jurisprudence, should make a contribution to the well-being of workers and see to it that, so far as possible, they should exercise their callings without harm. So I for my part have done what I could and have not thought it unbecoming to make my way into the lowliest workshops and study the mysteries of the mechanic arts."

In the course of carrying out his resolve Ramazzini inquired into the conditions of work and the occupational diseases of the following types of workers: miners of metals, gilders, healers by inunction, chemists, potters, tinsmiths, glass-workers and mirror-makers, painters, sulphur-workers, blacksmiths, workers with gypsum and lime, apothecaries, cleaners of privies and cess-pits, fullers, oil-pressers, tanners, cheese-makers and other workers at dirty trades, tobacco-workers, corpse-carriers, midwives, wet-nurses, vintners and brewers, bakers and millers, starch-makers, sifters and measurers of grain, stone-cutters, laundresses, workers who handle flax, hemp, silk, bathmen, salt-makers, workers who stand, sedentary workers, Jews (*i.e.*, old-clothes-men), runners, grooms, porters, athletes, those who strain their eyes over fine work, voice-trainers, singers, etc., farmers, fishermen, soldiers, learned men, nuns, printers, scribes and notaries, confectioners, weavers, coppersmiths, carpenters, grinders of razors and lancets, brick-makers, well-diggers, sailors and rowers, hunters, soap-makers.

As the final result of his prolonged and arduous researches, we find, among other wise counsels, this striking addition to the Hippocratic art: " When a doctor visits a working-class home he should be content to sit on a three-legged stool, if there isn't a gilded chair, and should take time for his examination; and to the questions recommended by Hippocrates, he should add one more—What is your occupation?" Ramazzini, as I have already remarked, is a very able writer. Did ever a man announce with more point, or with less fuss, a revolutionary innovation? In one innocent-sounding sentence he characterizes and supersedes the medical science and the medical practice of two thousand years.

The Hippocratic medicine, we are informed by

all competent inquirers, rested on the concept of a balance between the living organism and its environment. It regarded sickness as an effort to restore a disturbed equilibrium, and the duty of the physician was to co-operate with nature in her efforts to secure a readjustment. Therefore the Hippocratic doctor, who was frequently, perhaps even normally, itinerant, was taught to study, as he came to each new locality, the major features of the environment of his future patients. This is the subject of *Airs Waters Places*. As the title indicates, it was the natural features of the place he was taught specially to observe—the climate, the situation, the quality of the water. He was also given hints as to the kind of constitution he might expect to find in the inhabitants of a town living under conditions of Oriental despotism as contrasted with those enjoying the blessings of Greek liberty. That is to say, even the political environment of the patient was to be taken into consideration by the Hippocratic doctor. Historians have been very properly impressed with the comprehensive outlook of this ancient medical manual. But now, with Ramazzini to tell us what to look for, we see at a glance where it is deficient. Professing to be a treatise on environment, it omits what may properly be described as the most important element in the environment from the point of view of health and disease—the regular occupation of the man. The occupations which Ramazzini studied were not so very different from those practised by the Greeks. In Athens and in Corinth, as in Venice, they had their miners, their potters, their smiths, their fullers, their tanners, their midwives and wet-nurses, their bakers, their stone-cutters and laundresses, their carpenters, porters, fishermen, peasants, and the rest. But there was no one who examined into their typical complaints and attempted to suggest remedies for them. Instead we have the picture of the slave-doctor skipping from patient to patient without time to make a thorough examination of any, or of the artisan who demands a rough and ready cure because he has not leisure for a treatment that requires time and care.

When we ponder these facts it becomes, I think, clear that the Hippocratic medicine was already limited in its application to a section of the people. A treatise like *Airs Waters Places* was written for citizen doctors with citizen patients in view, and those too of the leisured class. If anyone should doubt the truth of this judgment I recommend him to turn to the four books of the Hippocratic treatise called *Regimen*. The author of this much-admired and very important treatise develops a theory that health depends on a balance of food and exercise. But the foods which he discusses hardly suggest the diet of a potter or a peasant, and the exercise which he recommends has nothing to do with work. Thus it would be a mistake to suppose that beef, goat, kid, pork, mutton, lamb, ass, horse, dog, puppy, wild boar, deer, hare, fox, and hedgehog all formed a normal part of the diet of the working man, slave or free, any more than doves, partridges, pigeons, cocks, turtles, geese, ducks, and other marsh or river fowl. And it would equally be a mistake to suppose that the following counsels as to exercise were addressed to a working-man: " Exercises should be many and of all kinds; running on the double track increased gradually; wrestling after being oiled, begun with light exercises and gradually made long; sharp walks after exercises, short walks in the sun after dinner; many walks in the early morning, quiet to begin with, increasing till they are violent, and then gently finishing."

The following advice also seems not to be addressed to the worker: " These patients ought to take their baths warm, to sleep on a soft bed, to get drunk once or twice but not to excess, to have sexual intercourse after a moderate indulgence in wine, and to slack off their exercises, except walking." This was the type of medicine which offended the taste and the good sense of Plato.

As I have explained in the first part of this essay, it was a long time before the prejudice against manual labour operated to depress the status of the surgeon to such a degree that the practice of anatomy died out and medicine in consequence ceased to be a scientific discipline. But the effects of the prejudice were felt in other departments of the medical art much earlier and with much worse results. For as soon as the class-divisions of ancient society had fully established themselves, then the care of the health of the working population ceased to be the concern of the exponents of scientific medicine, with the result that the whole problem of health and disease, in so far as it is connected with the occupation of the working population, fell out of consideration. In these circumstances alone is it conceivable how an eminent scientist like the author of *Regimen* should consider the problem of health on the assumption that the patient had nothing to do but to eat, drink, and amuse himself. Only because the narrow basis of this type of medical science has not been clear to modern historians has it been possible to describe the author of *Regimen* as the Father of Preventive Medicine. He in no way deserves such a title. Much more fittingly could he be described, in the spirit of the Platonic attack, as the Father of Valetudinarianism.

Furthermore, the development of medicine along these lines made it useless in relation to the needs of the mass of the population, even on those occasions when it was thought desirable to attend to them. This is another of the lessons that can be learned from Ramazzini. Let us listen to him on the Hippocratic art as applied to the Italian peasantry in his own day. It is a fair specimen of his style. He begins with a quotation from Virgil:—

> " ' O fortunatos nimium, sua si bona norint, Agricolas.'
>
> So in olden times sang the prince of poets. And his words were perhaps applicable to that

ancient race which ploughed its fathers' fields with its own oxen; but they are not so true of the farmers of our day who work unremittingly on another's farm and must struggle at the same time with dire poverty. And with what result? The diseases by which the agricultural population, at least in Italy, and especially on either bank of the Po, are wont to be attacked are pleurisy, inflammation of the lungs, asthma, colic, erisypelas, ophthalmia, quinsy, tooth-ache, and dental decay. The exciting causes are two: the weather and the wretchedness of their diet. . . . The mistakes that I observe in the treatment of this class of men are many, and they arise from this fact that the peasantry are supposed, on account of their tough constitutions, to be able to endure strong remedies better than city folk. But I for my part cannot withhold my pity when I see the wretched peasants brought in on all sides to the public hospitals and entrusted to the care of young doctors just out of school; for they wear them out by strong purges and repeated bleedings, without any regard to the fact that they are quite unused to these strong remedies and have weak constitutions on account of the labours they have undergone. This is the reason why many of the peasantry prefer to die in their huts rather than to bid adieu to life in the hospitals, with their veins drained of blood and their bellies scoured by purges. As harvest ends every year in the Roman countryside the City hospitals are filled by a throng of ailing harvesters; and who can say whether Death with his scythe or the phlebotomist with his lancet takes the richer harvest of their lives?"

Again, of the brick-makers he writes:—

"Workers of this sort are mostly drawn from the

peasant class; so, when they are attacked by fever they betake themselves to their huts and leave the affair entirely to nature; or else they are carried off to hospitals and there are treated, like everybody else, with the usual remedies, purging and venesection. For the doctors know nothing of the mode of life of these workers, who are exhausted and prostrated by unceasing toil."

And then he adds the sensible advice:—

"For these wretched workers the best remedy would be a fresh-water bath at the earliest stage when they begin to have fever; for their bodies are rough and dry with dirt, and by moistening the skin and opening the pores the fever would be given an outlet."

Such is the spirit and such is the content of Ramazzini's reform of the Hippocratic art. More than two thousand years lie between Ramazzini and his great predecessor who taught: "Where the love of mankind is, there is the love of the art." The long lapse of time makes one wonder whether it is not quite erroneous to understand the Hippocratic aphorism, as I myself have been prone to understand it, as if it were equivalent to saying: "Where the love of the art is, there is the love of mankind." In fact, we must understand that, though in classical antiquity it is possible to speak of the rights of the citizen, it is hardly possible to speak of the rights of man. A long development, not primarily of man's nature, but of his control over inanimate nature, was requisite before even the most far-sighted could venture to urge the desirability of extending medical attention to every level of the working population. Another two hundred years were to elapse before any Government organized such attention and set forth in its Constitution that the free enjoyment of medical aid was a basic right of the individual.

I now turn to the third and last of my topics—

namely, the invasion of medical science by *a priori* philosophic concepts. This process, in my opinion, accompanied the transformation of the healing art from a handicraft passed on by apprenticeship into a liberal art acquired through the medium of books and writing.

Here, too, I shall take a text from Vesalius. The anatomical plates with which Vesalius adorned the *De Fabrica* constitute a landmark in the history of anatomy and still excite admiration. It is matter for surprise, then, to observe that in the *Preface* he feels obliged to defend the preparation and publication of these plates. Detractors, we are given to understand, had seized the occasion of their appearance to accuse Vesalius (Vesalius of all men!) of wishing to substitute his illustrations for first-hand acquaintance with the body in dissection. His rejoinder is of interest for the early history of medicine. " Assuredly," he writes, " if the practice of the ancients had lasted down to our day—namely, to train boys at home in carrying out dissections, as in making their letters and in reading, I would gladly consent to our dispensing not only with pictures but with all commentaries. For the ancients only began to write about dissection when they decided that honour demanded that they should communicate the art, not only to their children but to strangers whom they respected for their virtue. For as soon as boys were no longer trained in dissection, the inevitable consequence at once followed that they learned anatomy less well, since the training had been abolished with which they had been wont to begin in youth. So much so that, when the art had deserted the family of the Asclepiads and had been now for many centuries on the decline, books were needed to preserve a complete view of it."

So far Vesalius. It remains to ask whether there is any justification for his point of view. Is it true that medicine, when it was a handicraft orally transmitted to boys, was in a flourishing condition and that it was only after medicine had been for centuries on the decline that it began to be committed to writing? The answer would appear to be that there is some substance in what Vesalius says, but that his judgment needs to be reformulated in the light of modern knowledge.

With the progress of modern archæology in the last couple of generations the whole problem of the origin of civilization, and of the arts of civilized life, has taken on a new complexion. It is now reasonably clear that civilization owes its rise to half a dozen fundamental inventions made in the region of the Fertile Crescent in the period from about 6000 to 4000 B.C. It was because man learned to control the production of food by agriculture and stock-raising, to store his supplies in clay pots, to build for himself houses of brick and stone, and to master the craft of the smith, that the complex mode of life which we call civilization became possible. Then the new needs of civilization called writing into existence. Simultaneously society tended to divide into a labouring and an administrative class. The practitioners of all the arts and crafts which had created the surplus which made civilization possible gradually came to form the lower strata of society. This is the process described by Herodotus when he says "those who learn a craft are held in less esteem than the rest of the citizens." This was more true of some crafts than others. The smith, the potter, and the peasant sank lower and lower in the social scale. But the scribe became an adjunct of the administration. The lore of the smith, the potter, and the peasant shared in the contempt which was felt for the man himself; but whatever was written was esteemed.

In these conditions society in time lost all true sense of its own origins The inventions of the fundamental arts, man's chief title to pride, were ascribed either to gods or philosophers. To Homer Aesculapius was a man, to Plato a god. The introduction of the fiction of the divine founders of the arts kept pace with the degradation of their practitioners. It was the opinion of the Stoic philosopher Poseidonius, in the second century B.C., that all the fundamental discoveries—agriculture, the potter's wheel, spinning, weaving, carpentry, metallurgy, and architecture—were made by the philosophers and handed over to slaves. The ingenuity required for their invention was too great for the slave, the drudgery of their exercise too lowly for the philosopher. The modern opinion is, however, that both philosophers and slaves were themselves the products of the first industrial revolution. The arts and crafts which Poseidonius presumed could only have been invented by philosophers were, in fact, the material basis of the first appearance of the genus philosopher.

It is from this point of view and in this social context that we must consider the most striking product of early Greek scientific writing, the Hippocratic treatise called *On Ancient Medicine*. The purpose of the writer of this fifth-century treatise was to protect the tradition of what he, even at that early date, calls Ancient Medicine from the dangers which threatened it from the empty speculations of certain natural philosophers. Vesalius, I feel sure, had this treatise in mind when he said that the medical art had been on the decline for centuries before it was committed to books. And though it would surely be a mistake to see only loss in the process by which the medical art came to be transmitted by writing, Vesalius would appear to have much justification for his opinion. For the treatise *On Ancient Medicine* is, in effect, a discussion of the dangers that threatened medicine in its transformation from a handicraft into a liberal art. It is the plea of a skilled manual worker against the theorizer who has no practical acquaintance with his subject. For him the healer is still known by his ancient and honourable designation of *demiourgos*, or public servant of the clan. The art he seeks to protect is an age-old tradition whose origin long antedates the birth of civilization.

The treatise begins with a protest against the intrusion into medical theory of the philosophical notion of the Empedoclean school. Empedocles had recognized four kinds of matter: Earth, Water, Air, and Fire; and he had further analysed these Elements, as they were called, into combinations of four Principles: the Hot, the Cold, the Wet, and the Dry. Certain physicians, attracted by this analysis, wished to apply the new philosophy to the art of healing. They sought to reduce all the causation of diseases to the excess of one or other of the four Principles and to cure it in each case by the application of the opposite Principle. What has our humble practical healer got to say in reply to this?

The reply is simple and crushing. Suppose, he says, your philosophical doctor diagnoses his patient as suffering from an excess of the Principle of Cold, he will presumably recommend as a corrective a dose of the Hot. But the patient, whose experience has never presented him with the Hot in isolation, will at once ask: " What hot *thing* ? " In response to which the philosopher will be reduced to talking nonsense or recommending some familiar *thing*. But no matter what thing he recommends it will have many qualities beside heat, many of which will be of much more importance than heat for the health of the patient. For while the maintenance of a proper temperature is in large measure an activity of the living organism, other qualities of food, like sweetness or bitterness, have a greater effect on the health. The philosopher is accordingly recommended to keep his empty postulates for speculation about things in heaven or under the earth, but not to bring them into the sphere of medical science where everything must be put to the test of experience.

The writer then gives a sketch of the growth of medicine which is remarkable for its historical imagination. He regards medicine as having begun when man adopted a different diet from that of the animals. The refinements since adopted in the diet of invalids in comparison with the diet of the healthy are a continuation of the earlier process. And research is still going on and progress is still being made. But neither in the past nor in the present is the medical art the creation of gods or philosophers. It is the result of the accumulated experience of countless generations of men who have busied themselves with the problems of health and disease while ministering to the needs of their fellows. *They* are the makers of the medical art, and their efforts will continue to produce results so long as they stick to the tried and tested method which experience has taught them.

Two points in his argument are specially relevant to the topic I have in hand. The first is the strong emphasis the writer lays on the view that the true doctor is a *cheirotechnes* and a *demiourgos*; that is to say a manual worker and public servant. We shall be surely wrong in our interpretation of his argument if we do not understand him to imply that these attributes are the hall-mark of the ancient tradition of scientific medicine. He is, in fact, defending medicine not merely against a new kind of theory, but against a new kind of man. The art of medicine, as he understands it, had grown up in a type of society in which the names *cheirotechnes* and *demiourgos* were titles of respect; it is threatened by the emergence of a new type of society in which these names carry a social stigma. The flourishing city-states of the Greek world had, in the fifth century, developed a brilliant literary culture which catered for the needs of the leisured class which was everywhere managing to dissociate itself from the productive life of society. Brilliant speculations like those of Empedocles spread rapidly throughout the Greek-speaking world and formed an intellectual stimulus for a far-flung public eager for every new thing The doctrine of the Four Elements, propounded in Agrigentum in Sicily, was soon drawing fashionable audiences in the lecture-halls of Miletus and Ephesus. These facts are of great interest for the historians of ancient Greek culture. But what we are privileged to read in *On Ancient Medicine* is a more important, a more sacred thing. It is the earnest protest of a man who has to defend a scientific discipline and a public function against the excessive importance attached to the fashionable chatter of the philosophic salons. The serious thing, he says in his opening sentence, is not that these philosophers are wrong, but that they are wrong in regard to an art which all men need at the most important crises in their lives, and whose craftsmen and practitioners they honour highly if they find them good.

The second point I wish to stress is closely connected with the first. There has been very general appreciation of the penetrating criticism, by the writer of *On Ancient Medicine*, of the Empedoclean doctrine of the existence of an absolute Hot, Cold, Dry, and Moist. But the author of *On Ancient Medicine* protests not merely against the uselessness of this analysis when put to the test of medical practice, but against its narrowness and ignorance. This note is struck in the opening sentence and recurs throughout the treatise. For him the famous Empedoclean Opposites are a poverty-stricken handful of empty abstractions. His is the first voice in history to be raised in championship of the teeming riches of positive science as against the barren emptiness of metaphysics. For him the qualities of things which affect a man's health are not three or four. They are infinitely various and infinitely subtle. "I know," he protests, "that it makes a difference to a man's body whether bread be of bolted or unbolted flour, whether it be of winnowed or unwinnowed wheat, whether it be kneaded with much or little water, whether it be thoroughly kneaded or unkneaded, whether it be thoroughly baked or underbaked, and there are countless other differences. And the same applies to barley. The properties of every variety of grain are powerful and no one is like another. But how could he who has not considered these truths or who considers them without learning know anything about human ailments? For each of these differences produces in a human being an effect and a change of one sort or another and upon these differences is based all the dieting of a man, whether he be in health, convalescent, or ill." And from this the writer proceeds to supplement the handful of Empedoclean concepts with a list of others more relevant to medical science—in foods, such qualities as sweetness, bitterness, acidity, saltness, insipidity, astringency; in human anatomy, the shapes of the organs; in human physiology, the capacity of the organism to react to an external stimulus. Such is the abundant richness of ideas, derived from the practical experience of one who uses his hand in healing, with which the fifth-century Hippocratic doctor overwhelms the pretensions of the philosophical physician whose theory rests on empty postulates.

This was the temper that saved Hippocratic medicine and made it, of all the sciences pursued by the Greeks, the nearest in outlook and spirit to modern science. From the earliest days, when the art of medicine was no more than a handicraft taught by a master to apprentices, there survived a tradition of learning directly from nature which saved medicine from the fate that overtook other branches of Greek science. The ancient doctor learned to understand the therapeutic rôle of food, drugs, and exercise. He was cook, apothecary, and masseur. He acquired skill in arresting the flow of blood from wounds, in applying bandages, in making splints for broken limbs, in preparing poultices of flour, oil, and wine, in adjusting dislocations. Together with manual dexterity went that alertness of the senses and that capacity for direct observation of nature which are the glory of Hippocratic medicine. Not only does the Hippocratic doctor advise the student to " practise all the operations, performing them with each hand and with both together . . . the object being to attain ability, grace, speed, painlessness, elegance, and readi-

A STUDY IN GREEK MEDICINE 51

ness "; he also tells him, when attempting a diagnosis, to use all the senses—sight, touch, hearing, smell, taste—as well as intelligence. Such was the temper of Greek medicine, coming down from the earliest times, lasting, at least in some degree, through all the vicissitudes of Greek society and still active, at least to some degree, in old Galen, who was reluctant, even in extreme old age, to let his slaves dissect the monkeys on which he made his observations. Throughout the doctor remained a manual worker, and his head worked to excellent purpose because it worked on material supplied by the hand.

How different was the fate of physics and chemistry! Here the Aristotelian view of matter acted as an insuperable barrier to progress. Accepting the Empedoclean elements, Earth, Water, Air, and Fire, Aristotle taught that an identical substratum, matter, underlay them all. All the differences came from the forms. Earth was cold and dry; Water cold and wet; Air warm and wet; Fire warm and dry. This qualitative analysis made all progress in chemistry impossible. It was almost two thousand years after Aristotle that the fundamental postulate of modern chemistry was explicitly formulated; that is to say, the belief in the existence of definite bodies capable of being isolated by suitable procedures and recombined to form new compounds. Paracelsus may appear a very muddled thinker beside Aristotle. His salt, sulphur, and mercury may have corresponded to no substances that have ever existed. But by the very fact that he was trying to break matter down into elementary substances, and not into qualities, he made it possible for experiment to be fruitful and for chemistry to be born. But two thousand years before him the author of *On Ancient Medicine* had been ridiculing the Empedoclean conception of matter. Two thousand years before him medicine had arrived at the standpoint of a strictly positive science. Two thousand years is a long time. What is the explanation of the time lag?

Before answering this question let us define it more closely. The author of *On Ancient Medicine* tells us that the point of view of the philosophers was that you could not understand medicine unless you first understood the nature of the universe. To this he makes the blunt reply that the very reverse is the truth. You cannot understand the universe without studying medicine. For there is no test that can be applied to the statements of the philosophers, while the statements of the physicians are being tested every day in practice in matters that fall within the experience of every man. If the medical practitioner could give so clear an answer to the presumptuous claims of the philosopher, why was there no early chemist to do the same? If the student of diet could pronounce the doctrine of the Hot, the Cold, the Wet, the Dry to be jejune and narrow, an insult to the inexhaustible variety of organic nature, why was there no investigator of inorganic nature to make a similar defence of his own science?

The answer I take to be this. The author of *On Ancient Medicine*, in proclaiming the rich variety of organic nature, had behind him a body of knowledge derived from direct contact with nature. Who could have had any similar body of knowledge of inorganic nature derived from direct experience? The answer can only be: the potter or the smith. For them, to be sure, the qualities of the materials they worked with were not exhausted by the Hot, the Cold, the Wet, the Dry, which exercised the tongues of generations of philosophers. For them matter was something much more rich and wonderful. It was malleable, mouldable, friable, fusible, soluble, insoluble, porous, impervious, a good conductor of heat or a bad conductor, elastic or inelastic, bendable, breakable, polishable, liable to tarnish or not, capable or incapable of taking a cutting-edge, and a host of other things. And if one succeeded in making things that were not normally found in nature, like bronze, one did so not by isolating and combining qualities, but by mingling substances. The smiths and the potters, who knew these things, were the pioneers of chemistry in early times. Why were they unable to defend the sciences that were implicit in their crafts? Their status at first was not lower than that of the healer. Like him they were *cheirotechnae* and *demiourgoi*, handicraftsmen working for the community. Why, then, did they not play the same rôle as the healer in the development of science in early times?

The answer would appear to be that their crafts, sooner than most and more completely than most, fell under the ban of social contempt. Theirs were the *banausic*, or mechanical occupations *par excellence*. Theirs were the crafts which Aristotle defined as being necessary for the existence of the city, but as disqualifying their practitioners for citizenship.[10] Under these conditions the knowledge of nature which they and they alone possessed could form no part of the speculation on the nature of things current in polite society. The development of the science of chemistry was a social impossibility.

But while the *polis*, or city, early achieved considerable success in expelling from its midst the practitioners of the banausic arts, it could not expel the healer, craftsman though he was, for the material on which the healer worked was the citizen himself. True, society succeeded in withdrawing from the care of the scientific doctor the care of the worker's health, thus inflicting on the healing art the gravest wound. But though slave might attend on slave, citizen attended on citizen, and one craft at least remained firmly installed in the citizen body and shared with it its rising literary culture. The healer was thus in a unique and privileged position. He retained the respect of society while remaining a manual worker.

As such, the doctor constituted the sanest and noblest figure of classical antiquity. He contributed to the body of ancient culture its soundest science and its soundest ethics. Not unnaturally, then,

Greek medicine occupied a position of peculiar privilege at the Renaissance and played a part beyond its own sphere in the creation of the scientific and the humanistic tradition of the modern world. It produced not only a Vesalius and a Ramazzini. In the sixteenth century medicine was a necessary part of a scientific education. Even a Copernicus studied it. And there was no ancient discipline better fitted to lead the groping mind across the bridge that separates scholasticism from modern science. And that, as I hope this paper has helped to make clear, was because no other ancient science presented such a happy blend of head and hand.

References

[1] Xenophon, *Oeconomicus*, iv, 203.

[2] In his book *Man Makes Himself*, a book to which this essay owes an obvious debt.

[3] A translation of this *Preface* by the present writer will be found in the Proceedings of the Royal Society of Medicine, Vol. xxv, No. 5 (July, 1932).

[4] Herodotus II, 167.

[5] Plato, *Politicus*, pp. 258, 259.

[6] Aristotle, *Politics*, III, 6.

[7] *Laws* 720 c, d.

[8] *Republic*, 406.

[9] Edited, with translation, by Wilmer Cave Wright, Chicago, 1940.

[10] Cf. *Politics*, 4, 4, 9 with 3, 5, 3.

III

DIODORUS SICULUS: UNIVERSAL HISTORIAN

BIBLIOGRAPHICAL NOTE

I wish to acknowledge a special debt to the following study:—

La Cité du Monde et la Cité du Soleil, J. Bidez, Paris, 1932. A more elaborate but less suggestive study of Iambulus will be found in *Geschichte der sozialen Frage und des Sozialismus in der antiken Welt*, Robert von Pöhlman, Munich, 3rd ed., 1925.

The English translations of Diodorus are the following:—

The History of Diodorus Siculus, done into English by H. C., Gent. (Henry Cogan), London, 1653.

The Historical Library of Diodorus the Sicilian, made English by G. Booth, of the City of Chester, Esquire, London, MDCC.

Diodorus of Sicily, with an English translation by C. H. Oldfather, London and New York, 1933 (in progress).

The following editions of Diodorus have been most valuable:—

Diodorus Siculus, ed. Peter Wesseling, Amsterdam, 1745. This is the only complete annotated edition.

Diodorus Siculus, Dindorf and Müller, Paris, 1878. This edition offers a convenient collection of the fragments of books xxxiv and xxxvi with a parallel Latin version.

Diodorus Siculus, Vogel, Leipzig, 1888.

Tarn, *Alexander the Great and the Unity of Mankind*, 1933; " Alexander, Cynics and Stoics " (*American Journal of Philology*, Jan., 1939), criticizes Bidez without sharing his clear understanding of Stoicism as a changing phenomenon in a changing world.

D. R. Dudley, " Blossius of Cumae " (*Journal of Roman Studies*, vol. xxxi, 1941), seeks to prove that Blossius was not a Stoic reformer but a Campanian patriot, basing his argument on the erroneous assumption that to support the reforms of Tiberius Gracchus was to be an enemy of Rome.

DIODORUS, to state in summary fashion the known facts about him, was the author of a " Universal History " in forty books, about one-third of which is now extant. He was a native of Agyrium, in Sicily, was born about 90 B.C., and lived on into the reign of

Augustus. He tells us that he took about thirty years in the composition of his history. He was, of course, Greek-speaking, but contact with the Romans in Sicily gave him an intimate acquaintance with their language. Thus he was enabled to utilize the resources, both Latin and Greek, of the libraries of Rome, which, according to his own statement, was his chief centre of study. He also tells us that he travelled widely in Europe and Asia in order to acquaint himself with the countries and peoples of which he wrote; but though it is certain that he was in Egypt (he reports as an eye-witness the lynching by an Egyptian mob of a Roman soldier who had accidentally killed a cat), it is difficult to feel confident that he was familiar with any countries except Sicily, Italy, and Egypt. He called his book an *Historical Library*, either to emphasize its comprehensiveness, or because he wished frankly to acknowledge the extent to which he had incorporated in it the writings of other men. It may be presumed that Diodorus was a man of independent means, otherwise he could not have commanded the leisure and wherewithal for travel and study. Probably he owned land in Sicily near his native Agyrium. It can further be said of him that among the rival philosophies of his day it was the Stoic creed, with its doctrine of the brotherhood of man, that won the allegiance of his sympathetic heart. To say that it claimed also the allegiance of his head would be to compliment too highly his meagre philosophical capacity.

The present is, perhaps, a not inappropriate moment for attempting to revive the claims of Diodorus to the attention of the English-speaking world. The editors of the Loeb Library, pursuing their beneficent task of supplying handy texts and translations of the Greek and Roman authors to the English world, have now made some progress with their edition of Diodorus. We may look to see the work completed in the next few years. It is surprising, however, to be reminded that the only previous efforts to make Diodorus the Sicilian speak English lie behind us at an interval of some two hundred years and more. Has this foreign voice, so long dumb among us, anything of importance to tell us to-day?

To Henry Cogan, gentleman, as he styles himself, who in 1653 translated into English the first five books of the history of Diodorus, that is to say so much of it as ran "from the first ages of the world until the War of Troy," the claim of his original to attention admitted of no doubt. "The History of Diodorus Siculus," he tells us, "hath been of so much repute with the most learned of all times, as he hath justly acquired a prime place amongst the best historians of former ages; yea he is preferred before them by Justin martyr, and Eusebius, who affirm him to be more renowned than them all: and truly it may be said of him, that what the whole universe is in comparison of one city, or nation, the same are his writings in regard of others; for whereas we can draw out of them, as out of a rivelet or little brook, the acts of but one city, or prince, we may out of him, as out of a great and spacious river, draw all that hath been done by the people of the habitable earth, and particularly by the most eminent states and flourishing commonwealths."

Henry Cogan, it will be evident from this specimen, had at command a prose style of much grace and dignity, fully adequate to the rendering of even a better writer than the Sicilian into English. It is to be doubted, however, whether he knew much Greek. At all events his version is most inaccurate. And the defects of his version, as well as its limitation to the first five books, are both to be ascribed to the same cause. They were "chiefly occasioned by an old Latin edition of Diodorus, whereunto the translator wholly applied himself, having at that time (without doubt) no better an edition to direct him."

This at least is the explanation of George Booth, "of the City of Chester, esquire," who in 1700 offered the first, and so far the only complete, version of Diodorus to the favour of the English public. George Booth was not prepared to accept Henry Cogan's version as satisfactory, but he is at one with him as regards the merits of their author and his claims on the attention of the English reader. He reminds us that Henry Stephen said of Diodorus that " among all the historians of antiquity that have survived to our day, if we consider rather the utility of the matter than the charm of the style, he stands out as the sun among the stars "; and he adds these further claims, that " amongst other excellencies of this author, he is peculiarly observable to have a regard and respect to the providence of God in the affairs of the world; and is the only ancient author that takes notice in the course of his history of the times wherein the most famous historians, philosophers, and poets flourished." [1]

Here, then, is the testimony of two Englishmen to the great value of Diodorus; and it would not be difficult to show that from the fifteenth to the end of the seventeenth century Diodorus was a living influence on English thought. But this is certainly not true to-day. He now belongs to that class of writers who are familiar to all students in footnotes and to few for their own sake. Nor do the historians of literature do much to excite one's interest in him. Bury, in his *Ancient Greek Historians*, gives him a page in which he quotes with approval his idea of universal history, but tells us that " he was quite unequal to the task." The routine practice in works of reference is to admit his indispensableness for certain periods and allude to his clear but pedestrian style. A Dublin professor, under whom I sat, claimed complete originality for him in one particular—his battle descriptions. He used to say that he had only one description for all battles—namely, trumpets, noise, brave deeds, numbers of dead, the inclination of Fortune to one side, and the flight of the other. Nor am I concerned to challenge the fairness of these strictures. As an original thinker, Diodorus does not count. Even the peculiar merits that earlier writers loved to claim for him now seem exaggerated. His championship of the action of Providence as a clue to history is a shallow and perfunctory contribution to a perplexed argument. Nor are his allusions to eminent figures in the world of intellect and art, refreshing though they be, sufficiently full or systematic to give his work the wide appeal of a history of culture. If there is one outstanding excellence I should like to claim for him, it is the sentiment of pity that pervades his work. But even this emotion is too little tempered with irony to be of the finest quality.

Nevertheless Diodorus is rich in interest, and the interest of his work is not unconnected with the mediocrity of the man. Mediocrity is perforce content to borrow, to reflect, to repeat what others have said; and in the special circumstances of Diodorus this was a very valuable function. The creative historian gives us his own construction of events. The feebler author, incapable of dominating his material, may bore us by his ineptitude, but, in his very incapacity, better mirror some aspects of his time. So it is with Diodorus. Living at the conclusion of the momentous epoch in the history of the Graeco-Roman world which saw a century of social convulsions issue in the transformation of the Republic into the Principate; actuated by an impulse to gather into one book the whole story of humanity; having still at command the complete treasure of Greek and Roman historical literature of which we have the fragments; but incapable of subduing this immense material into an orderly whole which would exhibit an original interpretation of the historical process, he turns here and turns there, borrows on this hand and on that, and leaves undigested, in his helpless pages, materials for a picture of the ancient world which are all the more significant for his failure to understand their significance. It matters nothing that Diodorus sometimes seems bewildered and ill at ease in his own historical library. Possibly he copied all the more diligently for that, and we have more leisure than he had to sort his materials.

From these materials I wish to extract only those bearing on one topic. Diodorus has something to say about every nation of antiquity. To quote his greatest editor, Peter Wesseling, one can find in him instruction with regard to the history, laws, and manners of the Egyptians, Ethiopians, Scythians, Assyrians, Persians, Greeks, Romans, Carthaginians, Gauls, and many other peoples. But the materials which I wish to select from the pages of Diodorus are those which throw an unfamiliar light on the social question in antiquity. Again and again there emerges from what he writes a criticism of the social conditions of his day, which he nowhere succeeds in developing systematically or in bringing to a point, but from which, apparently, he cannot long escape. It is as if he half consciously conveyed to us an element that pervaded the mental atmosphere of his day. What was this criticism of society of which Diodorus gives us so many glimpses? In what circles was it current? On what theoretical foundations did it rest? How far was it systematized? Did it find expression only in words? If it found expression in action, what was the scope and extent of this action? These questions suggest the theme of my essay.

The immediate source from which Diodorus derived his outlook on the world is not in doubt, and has already been mentioned. Stoicism was the chief influence that operated on him, as is plainly revealed in the preface to his work. There he tells us, in what is probably the most quoted passage of his writing, that " to write universal history is to be a servant of divine providence; for a universal history unites in one composition all mankind, who though separated in space are all brothers in blood." Here we may recognize the voice of Stoicism. Then in a most magniloquent sentence, of special interest as displaying the astrological foundation of the Stoic creed, he gives the reason for his claim that the universal historian is in a special sense the servant of divine providence. "Providence," he says, "wheels uninterruptedly throughout all time, composing into one harmonious whole the orderly procession of the visible stars and the lives of men, dispensing to each what Fate has decreed; and he who writes a history of the whole habitable world as if it were but one city makes of his labours a common archive of the record of mankind." This passage, the high-water mark of the intellectual achievement of Diodorus, is characteristic of his idealism, of his susceptibility to the lure of grandiose conceptions, and of his incapacity for coherent thought. But its chief interest for us at the moment is that it holds entangled in its skein of words the master conceptions of the Stoic creed; that is to say, not only the conviction that all men are brothers, but the theory that the whole universe is a unity in which the lives of men are indissolubly bound up with the actions of the stars by a sympathy which pervades all nature.

It was the practice during the greater part of the nineteenth century to discuss the Stoic philosophy as if it were a logical development within the domain of pure Greek thought. Then the recognition of the fact that a preponderating number of early Stoics, including the chief founders of the sect, were Orientals led to the view that the ethical peculiarities of Stoicism and its emphasis on duty were Semitic in origin; stress was laid upon race as a determining factor in Stoic thought; and comparisons between the Phoenician, Zeno, and St. Paul, the Jew, were the order of the day. But without denying the suggestiveness of this most interesting parallel, it may confidently be asserted that the supposed influence of Semitic blood is wholly inadequate to explain the originality, within the sphere of Greek philosophy, of the Stoic creed. The significance of the fact that the chief exponents of Stoicism came from the East resides not in the quality of their blood, but in the importation by them of a new system of thought.

Various lines of research have led scholars in recent years to the recognition of a profound influence on Greek by Oriental systems of thought; and this interpenetration of Greek philosophy with Oriental views is nowhere more pronounced than in Stoicism. Older than Greek philosophy and science was the science and philosophy of the valley of the Tigris and Euphrates. Here was the home of astrology. And though the modern adherents of this belief are in my opinion in error, there was a time, two thousand years ago and more, when acceptance of it might seem to be imposed by as strong an array of arguments as any other system could show. The Chaldean astrologers, basing themselves upon a systematic observation of the heavenly bodies, and utilizing a well-developed mathematical technique for the ordering of this material, had long anticipated the achievements in positional astronomy we are in the habit of crediting to the Greeks. But passing beyond this, they had erected, on a slender basis of observation and much unfounded speculation, a theory of the interdependence of celestial and terrestrial phenomena which experience has not confirmed. The central tenet of this system, which was passed on to the Middle Ages as the notion of macrocosm and microcosm, was the unity of the universe, the Cosmopolis, or city of the world, of which men were citizens indeed, but not the chief citizens. These were the visible deities, the sun, moon, planets, and the stars of heaven, whose orderly motions control the course of human destiny. The believers in this philosophy, or this religion, which has been called the most scientific religion of antiquity, practised reading the future of men from the starry map of the sky; but though the less worthy among them may have hoped, by having foreknowledge of their fate, to escape whatever in it did not please them, such was not the ambition of the nobler believers. For them happiness lay in conformity to the law of Cosmopolis, in gladly accepting the law of the universe. If a Zeno or a Cleanthes sought to read his future in the stars, it was so that he might attune his mind to whatever Fate held in store for him. This was virtue, this was happiness, this was wisdom; and it was this conception of the universe which lay behind the much misunderstood formula of Stoicism, life according to nature. Nature for the Stoic did not connote a return to the primitive; it meant obedience to the laws of Cosmopolis, the world state—laws not made by man, but revealed to him day and night by the luminous gods of the sky. Such plainly was the view of things that actuated our Sicilian landlord, Diodorus, when he conceived the idea of writing his universal history, and one of his invaluable contributions to history is the insight he gives us, in several passages, into the nature and influence of this system of thought.[2]

For though Diodorus does not fail to pay tribute to the efficacy of Greek philosophy to liberate men's minds from the power of superstition,[3] he also preserves for us a most striking criticism of the whole tendency of Greek philosophy, which is thrust home by an elaborate contrast with the system of thought of the Chaldeans, the originators and custodians of the astrological view of the universe. The Chaldeans, Diodorus tells us, are descendants of the most ancient inhabitants of Babylonia, and occupy in their country a position similar to that occupied by the priests in Egypt; that is to say, they are State-supported servants of the gods, free to devote their whole time to the pursuit of wisdom. The form of wisdom for which they are chiefly renowned is astrology. This study is traditional in the priestly families, being passed on from father to son from generation to generation. The leisure assured to this priestly caste, together with its hereditary character, has operated to produce a rapid advance of knowledge without disturbing the continuity and uniformity of tradition. With the

Greeks the whole position is reversed. Students approach a great variety of subjects without due preparation. Their philosophical training begins late and ends early, for when they have persevered for a little they are called away by the necessity of earning a living. Only a few really strip themselves for a serious philosophical training—namely, those who intend to make their living by teaching, and their practice is to innovate with regard to the most fundamental doctrines in defiance of tradition. The result is that the teachers are always founding new schools and bringing the most important questions into debate, while the pupils are bewildered and incapable of arriving at firm convictions.[4]

That a Stoic should institute a hostile comparison of Greek education with an external system should not be a matter for surprise. The first founder of Stoicism, Zeno, wrote, we are told, a treatise *On Greek Education*. Of its contents we are lamentably ignorant. But we are surely justified in inferring from its very title, and the circumstance of its being the production of a stranger, that it was in some sense a criticism from the outside. It was an estimate of the defects of Greek education from the point of view of some other and better system, just as his famous *Republic*, by the title of which he challenged comparison with Plato, was a rejection of the ideals of the Greek city-state from the standpoint of a citizen of the world. It seems, then, a most natural supposition that the passage of Diodorus we have been considering derives from the founder of Stoicism himself, and that the contrast between the fluctuating and individualistic philosophical tradition of the Greeks and the rigid orthodoxy of Chaldean astrology is a legacy to the Stoicism of Diodorus from its earliest days.

As the Stoicism of Diodorus, owing to its connection with Chaldean astrology, operated to produce a critical attitude towards Greek education, so also it influenced his outlook on the structure of society.

Here, again, Stoicism was from the outset in opposition to the fundamental ideas of the Greeks. Politically the Greeks were organized in independent city-states. Their religious system, adapting itself to the political, was equally particularistic. And their economic system rested upon a basis of slavery. In spite of the efforts of a few thinkers and publicists, the Greeks remained firmly attached to their tradition of religious and political particularism; while with the help of their philosophers they had secured a mental adjustment to the uncomfortable fact of slavery. Notwithstanding the obvious truth that slavery was often the result of unmerited poverty, of capture by pirates, or of being taken prisoner in war, it was maintained that the distinction between freeman and slave was not artificial, conventional, and accidental, but a law of nature. This miserable sophism was accepted by Plato and formulated by Aristotle in the famous description of the slave as an animated machine. Against all these conceptions Zeno, in his first work, the *Republic*, which was his manifesto, waged open war. Greek city-states were unimportant to him; there was one city, the City of the World, of which all men were citizens. Greek religion, with its local deities, meant nothing to him; the same gods ruled the whole universe—to wit, the sun, the moon, and the stars. The distinction between freeman and slave was to him an artificial one; virtue alone exalted one man above another; all men were citizens of the world, but the good alone were free, the rest slaves.

It needs little imagination to understand the effects such teaching might have in the public places of Athens, and then elsewhere throughout the Mediterranean world. The conception of the world-state might intrigue the political philosopher. The new conception of deity would find a welcome in quarters where the local deities with their dubious reputations had long been objects of attack. Here were matters worthy of debate by the intellectual leisured class. But the insistence that slavery was not natural was a different matter. This teaching appealed to a different stratum of the population, and touched ancient society in its sorest spot.

This championship of the slave gave early Stoicism a revolutionary complexion which became still more pronounced under its second founder, Cleanthes of Assos. Zeno had, it is true, been a foreigner, but he was a merchant. Cleanthes was equally a foreigner, and a proletarian. Beginning life as a pugilist, he came to Athens with a few shillings in his wallet, picked up his philosophy in the streets, and maintained himself while doing so by manual toil. He belonged to the class of society which in a timocracy is inevitably on the wrong side of the law. He had no visible means of support. He was a vigorous fellow, and society needed to be assured how he earned a living. He was haled before the court of Areopagus, and satisfied the authorities by summoning as witnesses the gardener for whom he drew well-water by night, and the miller's wife for whom he ground flour. The Areopagus, apparently satisfied with him, offered him a sum of ten mina, which he was forbidden by Zeno to accept. He regularly paid in to his master, Zeno, a portion of his wages. And when his humble way of life provoked criticism among men whose tradition was the Platonic one, that only a man of independent means could be a philosopher, he defended himself stoutly. He thrust out a handful of small coin and said: " Cleanthes could support a second Cleanthes, if he wished; but men of independent means live on others, and are yet but indifferent philosophers." Such was the man who, if I interpret his career aright, definitely associated Stoicism with the aspirations of the dispossessed element in society.

One of the items in the reformed Stoicism of Cleanthes was that he exalted the sun to the central position among the heavenly bodies which were the objects of the worship of the Stoics. This might appear to us an innocent and unimportant theological innovation. At the time, however, it is probable that its significance was great. There is abundant evidence that in many circles, where the religion of the stars had blended with aspirations after a juster society, the sun was looked upon in a special sense as the dispenser of justice, the guarantor of fairplay, the redresser of grievances, the one who held the balance straight. Already, in the code of Hammurabi, about 2000 B.C., we find that monarch claiming that he is the king of justice and that he derives this prerogative from the sun. And at the time of which we are now speaking—in the third century B.C.—the sun had become the centre of the millennial aspirations of the dispossessed among mankind. It was believed that at recurrent periods the sun-king would descend from heaven to earth to re-establish justice and make all men participators in a happiness without alloy. It would be natural enough for the wage-earning Cleanthes to share this devotion to the sun as the god of justice; and that his modification of the City of the World into the City of the Sun marked a definite alignment of Stoicism with practical movements for the equalization of wealth is confirmed by the career of his disciple Sphaerus.

At this period Sparta was the scene of a prolonged and violent effort at reform. The young Spartan king Agis paid with his life for his endeavour to reform his corrupt kingdom by a redistribution of lands, and by the admission of foreigners to the ownership of property and the rights of citizenship. His more determined successor on the throne, Cleomenes, actually succeeded in putting these reforms into effect, and in doing so relied on the advice and support of the Stoic Sphaerus. Sphaerus was thus the first, but not, as we shall see, the last, Stoic philosopher who aspired to direct the accomplishment of a drastic social reform.

We may now sum up the results of this inquiry into the social outlook of the early Stoics. From its connection with Chaldean astrology Stoicism had derived a belief in the brotherhood of the human race, based on the astrological view of the solidarity of the universe. This theory of the brotherhood of the human race implied a criticism of the institution of slavery from which the Stoics did not shrink. This rejection of slavery had a religious as well as a social aspect. It was connected with the worship of the sun, who dispenses his light and warmth equally to all, and would one day descend upon earth to establish his kingdom there. It is clear that it is because, as a Stoic, he was touched with the Stoic outlook on society, that Diodorus, in his history, exhibits the lively interest in the slaves which I now proceed to illustrate from his pages.

It would not be true, of course, to suggest that it was only those Greeks who came under the influence of foreign ideas who showed a disposition to criticize the institution of slavery. Euripides is an outstanding example of a Greek who rejected the sophistries that later satisfied Plato and Aristotle. And the Epicureans, equally with the Stoics, opposed the notion of slavery as a law of nature. Nevertheless it is significant that, for Diodorus, slavery was a blot not on civilization as a whole, but chiefly on the civilization of the Graeco-Roman world. Thus, in his idealized picture of the Indian caste system, he mentions with approval many features that sharply distinguish it from Greek society. He tells us, for instance, that the Indians, when they go to war among themselves, always respect the farmer and his lands, thus sparing the civil population the horror of famine. He tells us that there is no such thing as private property in land. He tells us that a strict social equality is established on the basis of equality of wealth, because " only a fool would try to establish equality before the law without also establishing equality of wealth." And then, with special emphasis, he tells us that " of their peculiar customs there is one instituted by their wise men of old which is the most noteworthy of all—to wit, it is ordained by law that no one among them shall be a slave." [5] It is, then, as one who believes in the actual existence of social systems not based on slavery that Diodorus describes the lot of the slaves in the Mediterranean world. Of these slaves there were two main types: the mine slaves and the predial slaves. We shall consider what he has to say about the mine slaves first.

There are two groups of mines to which Diodorus makes extended reference; they lie at opposite ends of the Mediterranean—in Egypt and in Spain. With regard to the mines of Egypt, he tells us that the Egyptian kings condemned to the mining of the gold three classes of person: criminals, prisoners of war, and those who had fallen under the royal anger and been unjustly accused and imprisoned. These last were sometimes accompanied to the mines by all their kith and kin, who were made to share in their punishment. Obviously drastic steps were necessary to secure a sufficient supply of labour. The labourers at the mines, he tells us, work in chains day and night, under a guard of soldiers, who are always foreigners so that the language barrier may prevent fraternization between them and their prisoners. Owing to the depth to which they penetrate the earth, they carry lamps bound on their foreheads. Different tasks are assigned to children, men of mature age, women, and old men. The workers have no opportunity to care for their persons; they lack even clothing to cover their nakedness. No man could look upon them unmoved by the extremity of their misfortune. No mercy nor respite is granted to the sick, maimed, or aged, nor to female disabilities. All are forced by the lash to persist at their tasks until they die of ill-treatment in the course of their forced labours. Owing to the hopelessness of their lot, death is looked forward to as the only release. Such are the sufferings that accompany the mining of gold. Nature herself proclaims, concludes Diodorus, that gold is troublesome to get, difficult to keep, a source of envy, and productive of as much pain as pleasure in its use.[6]

This sympathetic examination of the condition of a section of the lower stratum of society—a phenomenon very rare among the ancient historians that have managed to survive—is supplemented in many particulars by the description of the Spanish mines. These were mainly silver-mines, and were worked at first in a primitive way by the natives. Then came the Phoenician traders, bartering cheap goods for the valuable ore. Under the influence of this trade the Phoenicians increased in wealth, and the native Spanish miners in skill; but the mines continued to be worked in a haphazard and individualistic fashion until the Roman conquest of Spain. Then a flood of Italians descended on the mines, and the systematic exploitation of them by gangs of slave labourers purchased by large-scale capitalists began. Doubtless the new system of working the Spanish mines was developed, as many other Roman institutions were developed, under the influence of the system employed by the Ptolemies of Egypt. And it is of interest to note that it was an invention made by Archimedes in Egypt, his famous cochlea or screw, which served the Romans for pumping the water out of their Spanish mines. So the slaves made a rich revenue for their masters while they toiled underground in conditions which Diodorus describes in almost identical terms with those used of the Egyptian mines. All the miners would prefer death, he says, but the great physical strength of some protracts their agonies. Meanwhile much advantage has been reaped by the two exploiting peoples, " by the Phoenicians who have a genius for discovering sources of wealth, and the Italians whose genius is to leave nothing for anybody else." [7]

But if the condition of the mine slaves was desperate, they constituted on the whole a less distressing problem than the predial slaves; for the predial slaves were much more numerous. They worked the great ranches which had become the dominant feature of the agricultural life of Italy and Sicily by the middle of the second century B.C. A vivid light is thrown on their condition by the records we possess of the course of two great slave revolts which broke out in Sicily, the first of which lasted from 135 to 132 B.C., the second from 104 to 102 B.C. The memory of these tremendous events would still be living when Diodorus was growing up in the countryside which had been their theatre. And in the fragments that remain of his thirty-fourth and thirty-sixth books he gives us a precious narrative of these abortive revolutions. The narrative is precious not only for its record of events, but for the evidence it gives us of some serious effort to analyse the nature of the disease which threatened to destroy society.

The first of these revolts, Diodorus tells us, took people by surprise; but, he adds, it ought not to have done so, for it was produced by an obvious disease of society, the concentration of vast estates in the hands of a few wealthy families. These wealthy landowners appear to have lost all sense of proportion in the tide of prosperity that flowed in upon them. They purchased slaves, mostly from the populous east, in hundreds and thousands. They acted literally on the Aristotelian dictum that the slave is a living machine; and since, at the time, the machine was cheap, there was no need to take care of it. Replacement was cheaper than upkeep. The slaves were ill-fed, ill-clad, ill-housed in great barracks, and forced to work, often in chains, under the lash of the overseer. Some masters found it an economy to suggest to the half-naked slaves who looked after their vast flocks and herds, that they should clothe themselves by lying in wait for travellers and stripping them of their attire. The Roman district commanders would gladly have checked this abuse, which was making the roads impassable and abolishing all freedom of movement; but they were powerless. For the landlords belonged to the Roman equestrian order, and, as such, sat as judges in the courts before which the Roman magistrates would be summoned to give an account of their conduct. Government was powerless in the grasp of an insolent plutocracy. The hidden sore, which none could cure, at last came to a head. It is probable that the last intolerable torment and indignity that drove the slaves to the desperate expedient of revolt was the frequent resort to the practice of branding them.

The course of the revolt, which can only be given here in the most summary fashion, is eloquent of the state of society in which it could occur. The number of the revolted slaves, at first a mere four hundred, swelled within three days to six thousand, then to ten thousand; and they began to encounter successfully the Roman troops. It is difficult to form a clear idea of the amount of preparation that preceded the revolt, of the discipline of the slaves, and the quality of the leaders they threw up. But it is evident that they were something more than a mob. The first leader was a Syrian slave called Eunus. When, under him, the rebellion had already reached dangerous proportions, the landowners and the Government saw a gleam of hope in the fact that an independent revolt sprang up under a Cilician slave, Cleon. It was hoped that the two rebel armies would destroy one another. But the solidarity of the class front was sufficient to induce Cleon to submit unreservedly to the command of Eunus, and he brought with him five thousand followers to swell their common army. Within thirty days from the beginning of the rising the slaves had fifteen thousand men in the field. A general was despatched from Rome and took the field with eight thousand men. But Eunus, who had now raised his strength to twenty thousand men, encountered the Roman general in a regular battle and defeated him. The revolt spread like wildfire. Now, not twenty thousand, but two hundred thousand men were in arms against the Government. There were sympathetic revolts in other places. In Rome itself one hundred and fifty men raised the standard of revolt; in Athens over a thousand. There were risings also in Delos, where one of the principal slave-markets was, and in other places; all of which were promptly suppressed. In Sicily the revolt continued to prosper. Not only the countryside, but the towns, fell into the hands of the slaves, until almost the whole island had passed under their control. The struggle did not end for some four years, when at length the ordered government of Rome prevailed over the improvised slave state.

In the narrative of these events which Diodorus composed or borrowed the most remarkable feature is that the writer, while putting on record the excesses committed by the slaves, maintains his active sympathy for their just grievances and his championship of their essential humanity. His treatment of one incident in particular illuminates his point of view. At the outbreak of the revolt a landowner, Damophilus, and his wife, Megallis, both of whom had been notorious for the brutality of their treatment of their slaves, were taken by the slaves, and tortured and killed. But their daughter, whose sympathetic and tender concern for the slaves whom her parents abused had become a matter of common knowledge, was not only unmolested, but actively protected from all harm and conveyed to a place of safety. By this it was proved, comments Diodorus, that the excesses of the slaves were not the result of natural cruelty, but were intended as a requital of the injuries they had endured. By these words the true Stoic dissociates himself from the master lie of this epoch, that the slave was a different kind of creature from his owner.

With regard to the second slave revolt in Sicily, there is no need to summarize even its chief events. It will be more instructive to isolate one detail which throws light on the fundamental question: whether these revolts were merely blind reactions to intolerable oppression, or whether they contained in them some element that consciously aimed at establishing a new society. The most remarkable leader thrown up by this revolt was a Cilician named Athenion. Diodorus draws attention to an original feature of his programme. He did not accept all the runaway slaves who rallied to his standard into his fighting force. His prudent plan was to enrol in his army only the more physically fit, and to order the rest to remain at their productive tasks. This seems to suggest that the slaves seriously envisaged not merely reprisals on their oppressors, but the taking over of the management of the island. And this view is supported by an interesting fragment, referring to the first rising, in which the foresight of the revolted slaves is contrasted with the improvidence of the free proletariat. In that passage we read that, when the revolt occurred, the cleavage in the free population of Sicily between the rich and poor was so great that the poor openly rejoiced in the discomfiture of the rich and the success of the slaves. And we are further informed that when the slaves, looking to the future, carefully spared the villas, the property contained in them, and the stores of grain, and refrained from interfering with those proceeding to the labour of cultivating the ground, the city proletariat, driven by envy, and acting under cover of the slave revolt, burned the homesteads and plundered their contents. It seems a fair inference from these statements that, in the opinion of the writer, the outlook of the slaves was by no means limited to the exacting of reprisals on their oppressors, but that they looked to establish a permanent society under their own control.

If, then, we are justified, as I believe we are, in seeing in these revolts not merely the violent outbreak of desperate men, but at least in some degree a conscious effort to set up a new society, it would be of the greatest interest to know whether the new society had taken any definite shape in the minds of any thinkers in this epoch. Was there, we might ask, a revolutionary intelligentsia? And what expression, if any, did its ideas find? Our modern literatures contain innumerable examples of ideal societies. Ancient literature also, as everybody knows from the example of the *Republic* of Plato, was not innocent of Utopias. But Plato's ideal State left wholly out of account the fundamental problem of the slave revolts. What Plato was concerned with was to secure that all the governing class should be soundly educated according to the notions of the Academy. He was for reforming the State by giving all politicians a university education. But that the educated governing class ought to be free from the necessity of toil, and ought to be fed, clothed, and housed by the toil of a despised class of labourers, he never doubted. Utopias of the Platonic sort, therefore, could have no appeal to a mass movement of the toilers towards a new society. The question, then, is, Do we find anywhere set down in a systematic way a picture from the point of view of the under-dog of what the ideal society ought to be? Here, again, in his blundering way, Diodorus comes to our rescue.

Among the countries described by Diodorus are certain Islands of the Sun. Since he sandwiches his account of these islands in between his descriptions of Arabia and Ethiopia, it is obvious that he supposes himself to be describing a real place. This is perhaps the most striking example, in the whole of his history, of the stupidity of which he could be capable; for it is obvious that the source upon which Diodorus is here drawing was not a history, but an agreeable fiction. It is an account of an ideal society introduced, in the manner of Defoe and Swift, by a circumstantial narrative which had the singular fortune to deceive the universal historian. Criticism has left no room for doubt that the Utopia emanates from Stoic circles, which adds to its interest for us in the present connection and to our wonder at our historian's mistaking its true nature. It belongs in all probability to the second century B.C. The composition, whatever its original length may have been, has been condensed by Diodorus into a few pages, and of this scanty allowance of space some is wasted in reproducing the obviously fictitious narrative of the alleged discovery of the islands. Nevertheless the account we have of life in the Islands of the Sun is reasonably complete and is of absorbing interest. At the Renaissance it was widely familiar to European readers. Extracted from Diodorus, it was separately printed and published again and again. It influenced the *Utopia* (1516) of Thomas More as well as Campanella's *City of the Sun* (1627). But since it is unfamiliar to modern readers, I may be excused for offering an almost complete rendering of it.

The narrative of the discovery of the islands may be told in two or three sentences. There was a certain Iambulus, passionately addicted to learning as a child. On the death of his father, who was a merchant, he was obliged to follow the same profession. After various adventures he and a companion fell into the hands of an Ethiopian people, who made use of them as scapegoats for the purification of their land. They put them in a well-provisioned boat and told them to sail south, when they would come to a fortunate island and kindly people among whom they would have a blessed life. From this point I shall translate the story fully:—

> "The pair then sailed over a great expanse of sea and encountered many storms, but in the fourth month they came to the island of which they had been told, which was circular in shape and had a circumference of five thousand stades. As they drew near to the island some of the inhabitants came down and brought the boat to land. Then from all parts of the island they ran together, astonished at the arrival of the strangers, but treating them kindly and giving them of their supplies. Now the inhabitants of the island are very different both in their physical constitution and in their way of life from the

inhabitants of our own part of the world. They are all of one physical type and over six feet high; and their bones are flexible up to a point, springing back into shape like sinewy parts. Their bodies are exceedingly tender, yet in far better condition than ours; for instance, if they seize anything in their fingers it is impossible to force it from their grasp. They have not a hair on their bodies except for the head, the eyebrows, the eyelids, and of course the beard, but all the other parts of the body are so smooth that not the slightest down is visible. They are very handsome and well-proportioned. Their earholes are much wider than ours and are fitted with little flaps to cover them. They have a peculiar feature in their tongues, partly natural and partly artificially contrived. For their tongues are forked for a certain length, and they continue the cleft inwards so that the tongue is divided up to the root. Accordingly their utterance is very varied. They imitate not only every kind of human and articulate speech but the manifold cries of the birds, and in a word every variety of sound. What is most remarkable is that they can maintain two conversations perfectly at the same time, answering the questions of one person and discoursing to another on the circumstances of the moment; they employ one-half of the tongue for one purpose, the other for the other.

"The air of their land is perfectly tempered, for they live on the equinoctial line and are troubled neither by heat nor cold. Their fruits are in season all the year, so that, as the poet says,

'Pear on pear ripens, and apple on apple,
Cluster on cluster of grapes, and fig on fig.'

And always with them day is equal to night, and at noon nothing casts a shadow for the sun is directly overhead.

"They live in organized groups of clans, not more than four hundred relatives in each group. Their life is passed in the meadows, the land supplying abundant sustenance; for by reason of the excellence of the soil and the temperate air crops spring up of themselves beyond their needs. There is, for example, a prolific rush-plant, bearing abundant fruit like white vetch or pulse. This they gather and steep in warm water until it swells to about the size of a pigeon's egg; they then crush and knead it skilfully in their hands, fashioning loaves, which when baked are sweet and appetizing. There are copious springs, some of warm water suited for bathing and refreshing tired limbs, others of cold, very sweet and wholesome.

"The zeal for learning of the inhabitants is great, and their special study is astrology. Their alphabet expresses twenty-eight sounds but has only seven characters, each having four modifications. They do not write from side to side as we do, but vertically, from the top down. The people live to a great age, reaching the span of one hundred and fifty years as a rule without sickness. If a man becomes maimed or has any physical defect they compel him to depart this life by a law which admits of no exceptions. Their practice is to live a fixed number of years, and when they have completed this span they voluntarily depart by a strange death. For there is a special grass that grows in their island on which when one reposes he passes first into a mild oblivion and thence into sleep and death.

"They do not marry, but have their women in common, and the children that are born are brought up in common and equally loved. While they are still infants the nurses must frequently pass their charges round, so that not even the mothers can know their own children.

Thus since there is no jealousy among them there is no civil strife, and they keep their love of unity and concord throughout life.

" There are among them animals not large in size but very unusual in physical structure and in a certain property of their blood. In shape they are round and like tortoises, with two yellow stripes crossed upon their back. At the ends of the stripes are an eye and a mouth. Accordingly they have four eyes to see with and four mouths to eat with. But they have but one gullet to which all the food is brought, and their nourishment when taken down through this flows all into one belly. Like the belly all the other internal organs are single; but round about the periphery is a vast number of feet capable of carrying the animal in any direction. The blood of this animal has a wonderful property. It immediately glues together a cut in any living body, and a hand or other part that has been cut off can be fastened on again by it while the cut is fresh. This is true of any part of the body not connected with the vital centres.

" Each of the clans maintains a big bird of a peculiar sort, by means of which the infant children are tested to see what quality of spirit they have got. They mount the babies on the birds; off fly the birds; the babies who stand the aerial excursion are reared, but those who suffer from air-sickness or show fear they reject as not being likely to live to a proper age nor worth preserving for their spiritual qualities. In every clan the eldest man has the rule, like a sort of king, and all the rest obey him. But when he finishes his hundred and fifty years and, in accordance with the law, puts an end to his life, the next in age succeeds to the rule.

" The sea round the island, which has strong currents and ebbs and flows violently, is sweet to the taste. Of the constellations known to us the Bears and a great many others are not visible. There are seven islands in all, identical in size and at equal distances from one another, all employing the same laws and customs. All the inhabitants of these islands, although having a rich abundance of all things automatically supplied, are not self-indulgent in their enjoyments, but practise plain living and content themselves with a bare sufficiency of nourishment. Their meat and everything else they either roast or boil. Of rich sauces such as cooks concoct, or carefully varied condiments, they have no idea.

"As gods they honour the vault of heaven, the sun, and generally all the heavenly bodies. They skilfully catch an abundance of all sorts of fish and also hunt several varieties of birds. Fruits grow spontaneously in great plenty, and they have olives and vines of which they make abundant oil and wine. The snakes are large but quite harmless to man, and have edible flesh which is very toothsome. They make clothes from certain rushes which have in the middle a bright soft down. This they gather and mix with pounded oyster shells, thus making wonderful purple garments. There are other extraordinary animals, so strange as to be incredible. As for the people themselves, their whole way of life is very strictly ordered, although they do not take their meals together nor eat the same things. But definite days are appointed for the eating of fish, of fowl, of flesh, others when they have olives or other very simple relishes. They take turns in ministering to one another, in doing the fishing, and in exercising arts and crafts, and the public services also are administered in rotation, except by the very old. At their banquets and festivals are said or sung hymns and lauds to the gods, but most of all to the sun, by whose name the islands and their inhabitants are called.

"They bury their dead at low tide, covering them over with sand; when the tide comes in it buries them still deeper. The reeds from which they get their nourishment are a span in breadth, and they wax as the moon waxes and dwindle as it wanes. The water of their hot springs, which is sweet and wholesome, keeps its heat and never grows cold, unless cold water or wine is added.

"Iambulus and his friend abode seven years with them, and were then cast out against their will, as evil-doers bred in corrupt ways."

The islanders fitted up their boat for them and compelled them to depart. Thus after further adventures, and the loss of his companion, Iambulus returned to Greece and put on record the account of his sojourn in the Islands of the Sun.[8]

If we seek now to analyse the heterogeneous elements of which this utopian romance is composed, we may admit that certain details afford some excuse to Diodorus for supposing it to be historical. There is, for instance, the practice of writing vertically from top to bottom, and the plant that yields a bright soft down from which clothes are made. These suggest the East; and it is quite possible that these particulars may indicate actual acquaintance on the part of some traveller with the island of Ceylon. But this will not suffice to rescue Diodorus from the reproach of excessive credulity. Even his most devoted editor cannot here refrain from censuring Diodorus for seeking to adorn his history with trifles, the fictitious character of which is obvious.[9] Indeed, however delightful they may be as fictions, the story of the birds that are used to test babies, the animal with the magic blood that heals all wounds, and the warm water that never grows cold should have sufficed to warn even Diodorus that he was not here in the domain of history.

But even more remarkable than his ability to swallow

the marvels is his apparent insensibility to the utopian intention of the tale. On reflection it appears to me that Diodorus must have been so much drawn to the Stoic ideal of society that he was only too ready to believe that it had already materialized somewhere on earth.

In any case, of the real character of the fiction of Iambulus there can be no doubt. It is a Stoic Utopia exhibiting in the most unmistakable way the intimate connection between Stoic and Chaldean conceptions of the universe and society. The islands are the Islands of the Sun, and the inhabitants are the Sun men. Each island is, like the sun, circular in shape, and they are seven in number, to correspond with the sun, moon, and five planets. There is a plant on the island that waxes and wanes with the moon, a detail illustrating the sympathy observed, or imagined, to exist in Chaldean astrology between heaven and earth. Furthermore, we are told that the special study of the inhabitants is astrology; and that their worship is directed to the vault of heaven, the stars, and above all the sun.

Again, it is upon this astrological character of the society that its just constitution depends. It is because the inhabitants are Sun men, and worship the sun as god, that their society is based upon a sort of egalitarian communism. The islands lie upon the equator, a symbol of the equality that reigns there over all. The inhabitants are all of one type and size, and all live to the same age. But still more significant than these fancies are the details of their deliberate organizing of their communal life. Thus leadership in the various communities goes round in rotation according to seniority. There are no rich and no poor. There is no distinction between slave and free. Domestic tasks, and public duties, devolve in turn upon all; and all must take their turn at all the trades. There are no temples, for their gods are visible to all and live in temples not made with hands. And as there are no priests, so there are no police and no soldiers; for there is neither crime nor war, where all is ordered according to nature. Needless to say, there are no guardians as with Plato. Wisdom and leisure are no longer the privilege of a class, for a classless society has been achieved.

The fiction as we have it is a light one. I suspect also that, in the process of condensation it has undergone, some gaiety and high spirits have been squeezed out of it, as well as some sarcastic thrusts at the utopian dreams of the epoch. For I find it difficult to believe that the composition is wholly free of satiric intent. But we must surely also recognize, as the social reformers of the sixteenth and seventeenth centuries did, that it implies a very searching criticism of the evils of the day. Nor is such literature as this likely to be a mere academic exercise. Utopias are not as a rule composed out of the blue; they are literary products of a period of social upheaval; symptoms of an uneasy conscience in the educated classes. The fictions of Jonathan Swift are not innocent of allusion to the Ireland of his day.

Of this stirring of conscience in the governing class of Rome the Gracchan movement is the most familiar symptom. What the judgment of Tiberius Gracchus was on the Italy of his day we know from the speech of his which Plutarch has preserved: "The wild beasts," he cried, "that range over Italy have every one of them some hole or lair to shelter them; but the men who fight and die for Italy have nothing but the common air and sun; without hearth or home they wander about with their wives and children. Their generals appeal to them in battle to defend their tombs and their altars from the enemy. But the generals are in error. Not one of all these many Romans has an hereditary altar nor an ancestral tomb. They fight and die to maintain others in wealth and luxury; but though they are styled the lords of the earth not one of them has a single clod of earth that he can call his own." This is remarkable language for a Roman; one would think to read it that Tiberius had gone to school to the Stoics. And this is likely to be the truth. The passage should in all probability be put down to the inspiration of Stoic enthusiasm for social justice. For, like the reforming Spartan king Cleomenes, Tiberius had at his elbow a Stoic philosopher.

This remarkable man, Blossius of Cumae, had a career which affords us the most striking testimony we possess to the influence which Stoic ideals exercised, and inclines us to see in the attempted Gracchan reforms a distant echo of the note sounded by Zeno in Athens two hundred years earlier. Blossius the Stoic not only urged Tiberius forward with his programme of reform and nerved him at the crisis of his fate, but, when Tiberius had been slain by a senatorial mob, he withdrew to the other end of the Mediterranean, and threw in his lot with an army largely composed of slaves in revolt who were attempting to save the kingdom of Pergamum from incorporation in the Roman Empire. On the defeat of their cause he slew himself. Why this Italian should have cared so much for the cause of the Asiatic slaves as to give his life for it becomes somewhat clearer when we are told that these slaves had given themselves the same title as the inhabitants of the Stoic Utopia, the Island of the Sun. They were the Sun men, fighting for the cause of social justice. This was the allegiance which summoned the Stoic Blossius from defeat on one field in Italy to death on another in Pergamum.

His career, then, vividly illumines the movement in ancient society of which the history of Diodorus is another manifestation. As everybody knows, by the middle of the first century Stoicism had become the most popular philosophy in governing circles in Rome. It then no longer produced men, like Sphaerus or Blossius, concerned to give practical effect to the views that land is by nature common and men by nature free. These two principles were unacceptable to a society dominated by the owners of large estates worked by slave labour. On the question of *res mancipi*, that is the typical form of Roman capital, consisting of land and the slaves and cattle necessary to work it, Stoicism had to give way. Otherwise it suited the Roman character and circumstances to perfection with its inculcation of devotion to duty, and its universal gods so suitable for an empire. It is the interest of Diodorus that he seems to preserve for us echoes from the earlier Stoic period when its devotion was to the City of the World and not to the City on the Tiber.

References

[1] It would not be difficult to adduce further evidence of the esteem in which Diodorus was held by Englishmen in the seventeenth century and earlier. Thus the Latin version of the first five books, published in Bologna in 1472 and ascribed to the Florentine Poggio, was claimed in England as the work of an Englishman, John Free of the city of Bristol. See Guilielmus Burtonus, *Graecae linguae Historia*, London, 1657, p. 55; Brianus Twynus, *Antiquitatis Academiae Oxoniensis Apologia*, Oxford, 1608, p. 371; Anthony à Wood, *Historia et Antiquitates Universitatis Oxoniensis*, Oxford, 1674, vol. ii, p. 76. I know no sufficient reason why the claim of John Free to be the first translator of Diodorus into Latin should now be generally disallowed in favour of Poggio. The 1472 version was that employed by Henry Cogan.

Additional evidence of the interest taken in Diodorus in England in the seventeenth century is supplied by the poetry of George Herbert. His poem *Providence*, so strongly Stoic in outlook, is almost certainly indebted to the third book of the *Library* of Diodorus for certain curious features. The verse beginning " Thou hast hid metals " should be compared with Diodorus, book iii, chaps. 12–14. The extraordinary proof of the versatility of Providence offered in the line

Most things sleep lying, the elephant leans or stands

comes from the same book, chap. 27, pars. 1 and 2. While the striking lines

the Indian nut alone
Is clothing, meat and trencher, drink and can,
Boat, cable, sail, and needle, all in one

reproduce exactly the form of a similar sentence in chap. 21, par. 5: τὴν γὰρ αὐτὴν αὐτοῖς εἶναι τροφήν, ἀγγεῖον, οἰκίαν, ναῦν.

² For the view that " the chief cause of the peculiarities of the Stoical School is to be sought in the race of its founders," see *The Ethics of Aristotle*, by Sir Alexander Grant, 3rd ed., pp. 306 ff.

For the astrological background of the Stoic creed, see *La Cité du Monde et La Cité du Soleil*, J. Bidez.

³ Diodorus, book iii, chap. 6, illustrates the efficacy of Greek thought to conquer superstition by the following story. It was the practice of the Ethiopian priests at Meroë to maintain their control over the monarchy by ordering the successive kings to die at the time they thought fit. The kings, implicitly believing the sacerdotal claim to be the mouthpiece of the divine will, obeyed from time immemorial this injunction to commit suicide until in the time of Ptolemy II the Ethiopian king Ergamenes, having acquired a Greek education and therewith a philosophic outlook, defied the priestly injunction and asserted the royal authority by slaughtering the priests.

⁴ Diodorus, book ii, chaps. 29–31. With this passage should be compared the extract from the *De Finibus* that follows :—

" Physicae quoque non sine causa tributus idem est honos, propterea quod, qui convenienter naturae victurus est, ei proficiscendum est ab omni mundo atque ab eius procuratione. Nec vero potest quisquam de bonis et malis vere iudicare, nisi omni cognita ratione naturae et vitae etiam deorum, et utrum conveniat necne natura hominis cum universa. Quaeque sunt vetera praecepta sapientium, qui iubent *tempori parere* et *sequi deum* et *se noscere* et *nihil nimis*, haec sine physicis quam vim habeant (et habent maximam) videre nemo potest. Atque etiam ad iustitiam colendam, ad tuendas amicitias et reliquas caritates quid natura valeat, haec una cognitio potest tradere. Nec vero pietas adversus deos, nec quanta iis gratia debeatur, sine explicatione naturae intellegi potest." Cicero, *De Finibus*, book iii, chap. 22 (par. 73).

What this passage implies is the shifting of the whole proverbial wisdom and ethical doctrine of the Greeks on to a new foundation—a knowledge of the universe and the way in which it is run. And this new knowledge, as a comparison with the passage of Diodorus cited above reveals, is the Chaldean theory of man and the universe as bound together into an indissoluble unity, the theory of microcosm and macrocosm.

⁵ Diodorus, book ii, chap. 39, § 5–chap. 41, § 5.

The phrase, εὔηθες γὰρ εἶναι νόμους μὲν ἐπ' ἴσης τιθέναι πᾶσι, τὰς δ' οὐσίας ἀνωμάλους κατασκευάζειν, which contains so significant and familiar a thought, has fallen on evil days. The passage, which is correctly understood both by Henry Cogan and by George Booth, is rendered in the Loeb Library edition as follows: " since it is silly to make laws on the basis of equality for all persons, and yet to establish inequalities in social intercourse." This fatuous version has not been arrived at without help from the textual critics. For the οὐσίας of the

MSS. Dindorf, followed by Bekker, proposed to read ἐξουσίας; Capps, followed by Oldfather for the Loeb text, prefers συνουσίας. Emendation is entirely gratuitous.

⁶ Diodorus, book iii, chaps. 12–14.

⁷ Diodorus, book v, chaps. 35–8. With regard to the effects of the mine conditions on the health of the miners, his contemporary, the Roman poet Lucretius, tells the same tale with the concentrated force of his peculiar genius. "See you not, when men are following up the veins of silver and gold and searching with the pick quite into the bowels of the earth, what stenches Scaptensula (a town in Thrace where there were silver mines) exhales from below? Then what mischief do gold mines exhale! to what a state do they reduce men's faces and what a complexion they produce! Know you not by sight or hearsay how they commonly perish in a short time and how all vital power fails those whom the hard compulsion of necessity confines in such an employment!" *De Rerum Natura*, vi, 808–15.

⁸ Diodorus, book ii, chaps. 55–60. The fullest discussion of this Stoic Utopia is to be found in Pöhlman, *op. cit.*, pp. 305–24. It might, indeed, be complained that the treatment is too full, some of the efforts to equate details in Iambulus' account of the Islands of the Sun with points in the programmes of modern Socialists exhibiting little historical sense.

⁹ Diodoro paene succenseo, huiusmodi nugis historias suas distinguenti atque ornanti, says Wesseling.

IV

THE GODS OF EPICURUS AND THE ROMAN STATE

THE *Tusculan Disputations* is often described as an effort on the part of Cicero to introduce the study of philosophy to Rome. Cicero would like to make this claim himself. " Philosophy has lain neglected to this day and Latin literature has thrown no light upon it: it must be illuminated and exalted by me, so that, if in the active business of life I have been of service to my countrymen, I may also, if I can, be of service to them in my leisure " (I. iii).[1] But the description is not accurate, and the claim is not justified. For elsewhere in the *Tusculans* Cicero makes it clear that what had been lacking at Rome was not philosophy, but philosophy of a certain type. The advent of the Socratic schools, he tells us, had been delayed; but " to fill the gap left by the silence of the various upholders of the Socratic tradition came the voice of the Epicurean Gaius Amafinius, and by the publication of his works the crowd had its interest stirred, and flocked to the teaching he advocated in preference to any other, whether because it was easy to grasp, or because of the seductive allurements of its doctrine of pleasure, or possibly because, in the absence of any better teaching, they clung to what there was. After Amafinius again there came a number of imitators of the same system and by their writings took all Italy by storm, etc." (IV, iii, 6 & 7). And elsewhere again in the *Tusculans* we read that Romans of education and literary skill are to bestir themselves to wrest the palm of philosophy from the failing grasp of Greece and transfer it to Rome, not because there is no philosophy at Rome but because the wrong kind has prevailed. " For there is a class of men, who wish to be called philosophers and are said to be responsible for quite a number of books in Latin, which I do not for my part despise, for I have never read them; but as on their own testimony the writers claim to be indifferent to definition, arrangement, precision, and style I forbear to read what affords no pleasure. What followers of this school say and what they think is not unknown to anyone of even moderate learning. Inasmuch, therefore, as by their own showing they do not trouble how they express themselves, I do not see why they should be read except in the circle of those who hold the same views and read their books to one another" (II, ii, 5–7). It is evident, therefore, that there was, before Cicero wrote, an established and widespread tradition of Epicurean philosophy at Rome depending not only on Greek but on Latin books by many writers. And Cicero's aim might therefore more accurately be described as the effort to introduce into Rome not philosophy but a rival philosophy to Epicureanism.[2]

It might, however, with a superficial appearance of justice, be urged that the writings of the Epicureans hardly deserved the name of philosophy, and certainly did not deserve the name of literature, and that Cicero is therefore entitled to boast that the year 45 B.C., in which he wrote the *Consolatio*, the *Hortensius*, the *Academica*, the *De Finibus*, and the *Tusculans*, marks the beginning of philosophical literature at Rome. He might be entitled to this boast were it not that in 45 B.C. the *De Rerum Natura* of Lucretius was already some ten years old. That the author of the *Tusculans* should be putting himself forward as the founder of the philosophical literature of Rome ten years after the death of Lucretius is an act of presumption remarkable even for Cicero. When he wrote the words " Philosophy has lain neglected to this day, and Latin literature has thrown no light upon it," he might excuse himself to himself for his failure to mention Lucretius by the plea that he was referring only to prose. But at the bar of history he can not be acquitted of the charge of deliberately suppressing the greatest name in the history of philosophy at Rome. If he were sincere in condemning the others for their lack of style, surely here was his chance to welcome the great exception.

The problem of Cicero's silence on the subject of the *De Rerum Natura* where mention of it would seem inevitable has been emphasized afresh in a recent study by Mr. Carleton Stanley, President of Dalhousie University.[3] "How," he asks, "did Lucretius strike his contemporary, Cicero? An answer to that question reveals," he continues, "one of the most remarkable things in the whole history of European literature. Cicero's writings prove that he had not only read, but diligently conned the poem of Lucretius. Why, then, did Cicero deny, not once, but twice, and in the most emphatic manner, about ten years after Lucretius died, that he had ever read him? In *Tusculans* I, 3, after speaking about works on the Epicurean philosophy, he says: 'there are *said to be* many works on this subject in Latin, carelessly written.' 'Said to be' means, of course, 'I don't know them at first hand.' But in the third chapter of the second book he says it in set terms: 'There are said to be quite a number of books in Latin; these I have not read.' Munro points out that Cicero, though he dealt with similar themes and obviously knew the writings of Lucretius well, never mentions him by name except in the letter we have noted (Q. Fr. II. 9). . . . Martha adduces several possible reasons: Cicero's jealousy of the man who had supplanted himself as the foremost philosopher and poet in Latin, and so on, but surely he gives *the* reason when he says that Lucretius had already come to be considered dangerous and impious. In ten years Lucretius had joined the great army of the Unrespectabilities."

The problem here so strikingly presented is not novel, but will perhaps bear re-examination. The attitude of Cicero to Latin writing on Epicureanism is certainly strange and equivocal. In the famous letter to his brother Quintus, a few months after the death of Lucretius, he had spoken with enthusiasm of the "light of genius" that irradiated the *De Rerum Natura*, but ten years later we read that up till now no light had ever been shed upon philosophy by any Latin writing. In his correspondence with Cassius, in the very year in which he wrote the *Tusculans*, he jokes about the translations of technical terms to be found in the writings of Latin Epicureans,[4] which would seem to imply that he had some acquaintance with the books he denies he has ever read. In other words, in his private correspondence he admits to having read not only Lucretius but Catius;[5] in his published works he denies it. It does nothing to relieve our suspicion of insincerity that the strict Quintilian should have found the despised Catius quite a respectable stylist.[6] Nor does it seem fair to have attempted to ascribe the popularity of the Latin Epicurean writings to their doctrine of pleasure, when all the evidence is that these writers devoted themselves almost exclusively to the exposition of the physical side of the system.[7] The point is worth insisting upon, for although Gassendi, in the seventeenth century, knew better than to admit the evidence of Cicero on Epicureanism without close examination,[8] more recent critics[9] have inclined to accept what he has to say at its face value, as if he were as candid a soul as Lucretius himself. But this he was not; and in fact the attitude of Cicero to Epicureanism, by reason of its very lack of candour, throws much light on the spiritual atmosphere of this vital period in the history of human thought. Still more can this claim be made at the present moment, when new evidence has enabled us to form a better judgment of what the system of Epicureanism was in its totality when Cicero girt up his loins to do battle with it.

To Gassendi in the seventeenth century it was evident that Epicurus had taught a singularly pure religion, if a defective one. Drawing a distinction between the filial and the servile elements in religion, the servile being those concerned with the interchange of services between men and gods, the filial with pure devotion, Gassendi emphasized the fact that it is only the servile elements of religion that are lacking in Epicurus.[10] Even in the light of the evidence available to Gassendi it was therefore a problem why so many professedly religious thinkers in antiquity should have hastened to condemn Epicurus for atheism.[11] The new evidence makes the problem seem still more acute. As this evidence became available only since Bailey finished the last of his studies on Epicureanism,[12] and as it has been ignored by subsequent writers,[13] it seems desirable to discuss it at some length before returning to the question of Cicero's attitude to Lucretius.

Up to the appearance of the last of Bailey's studies the most important extant writings of Epicurus had been the three letters—to Herodotus, to Pythocles, to Menoeceus. In 1933 the existence of a fourth letter was revealed in the publication by Christian Jensen of *Ein Neuer Brief Epikurs*.[14] Jensen was engaged upon the task of reconstructing and interpreting the charred Herculanean fragments, and transcripts from the fragments, containing the work of Philodemus on *Vices*, when his patience and ingenuity were rewarded by the discovery that what he was piecing together was nothing less than a letter of the master Epicurus himself. Obviously such a discovery is of exceptional interest and importance.

Both the structure of the letter, which is a little complex, and the occasion of it, are made clear by Jensen's deft analysis. The beloved disciple of Epicurus, Metrodorus, had a brother, Timocrates, the Judas of the group. Timocrates had, on the recommendation of another disciple, Leonteus, been preferred to a post at the court of King Lysimachus of Lampsacus. At Lampsacus he had fallen away from the teaching of the Garden and joined a rival movement, the sect of the Epidaurians, followers of the god Asclepius, the god of health. Not content with apostasy, he had published a book in which the teaching of his former master and the life of the Garden were vilely slandered. Epicurus felt his position and that of his school to be so seriously threatened by this attack that it was necessary to defend himself by every means in his power. To this end he wrote to one Mithres, treasurer at the court of Lysimachus, and presumably in authority over Timocrates. The letter is not a direct appeal for help. It takes a curious form. Epicurus makes the god Asclepius arbitrator between himself and Timocrates; and the letter consists of the plea of Epicurus to the god and the speech of the god in reply. The address to the god is sufficiently remarkable. The reply is still more so, for the god not only acquits Epicurus of the charges laid against him by Timocrates, but also expressly assures him of the divine approval and protection.

But this does not end the story. It appears that certain expressions in this letter of Epicurus to Mithres were taken from their context, distorted, and made the basis for a fresh attack upon the writer for his pride. Leonteus, also resident at Lampsacus, was distressed by these charges, and referred the matter to Epicurus at Athens. Epicurus, in his reply on the subject of his attitude to the sin of pride, quotes the essential parts of his former letter to Mithres—namely, the address to the god and the god's reply, which had been the pretext for the accusation. It is the letter to Leonteus, containing the extract of the letter to Mithres, which Jensen has recovered and edited. The very complexity of the story, involving so many persons whose names and mutual relationships are independently known to us, facilitates and confirms the reconstruction and interpretation of the letter. Its date is not fixed more precisely by Jensen than the statement that it belongs to the latter part of the period 306 to 281 B.C., the years when Lysimachus was king.

The problem raised by the recovery of this letter can best be stated in Jensen's own words:—

" The discovery of the two speeches was for me a great surprise. For I believed that according to the teaching of Epicurus the gods do not trouble themselves about men, and I still read this opinion to-day in the latest expositions of his teaching. How is it consistent with this that Epicurus should write down a dialogue which he has held with Asclepius? And how can it accord with the spirit of his teaching that Asclepius should speak of the goodwill that certain of the gods have shown to Epicurus, nay, that he should expressly assure him of his care? "

Jensen has not been content to raise these questions; he has answered them. This he has done by showing how the newly discovered doctrine on the gods slumbered undetected in familiar Epicurean texts. In the most moving and beautiful of the extant writings of Epicurus, the letter to Menoeceus, the second paragraph runs as follows (I quote Bailey's version):—

" The things which I used unceasingly to commend to you, these do and practise, considering them to be the first principles of the good life. First of all believe that god is a being immortal and blessed, even as the common idea of god is engraved on men's minds, and do not assign to him anything alien to his immortality or ill-suited to his blessedness: but believe about him everything that can uphold his blessedness and immortality. For gods there are, since the knowledge of them is by clear vision. But they are not such as the many believe them to be. And the impious man is not he who denies the gods of the many, but he who attaches to the gods the beliefs of the many. For the statements of the many about the gods are not conceptions derived from sensations, but false suppositions, *according to which the greatest misfortunes befall the wicked and the greatest blessings the good by the gift of the gods. For men being accustomed always to their own virtues welcome those like themselves, but regard all that is not of their nature as alien.*"

In this translation, as Jensen's work makes clear, the italicized portion entirely misrepresents the thought of Epicurus. The fault is not Bailey's. It lies with the universal misunderstanding of the doctrine of Epicurus, helped in this instance by an interpolation made by Gassendi.

When Gassendi read the above passage in Epicurus, having in mind the Christian, and Platonic, idea of rewards and punishments, he supposed it was this conception that Epicurus was dismissing as a false supposition of the many. In the italicized phrase above, *the greatest misfortunes befall the wicked and the greatest blessings the good by the gifts of the gods*, the words *the good* were supplied by Gassendi. Omitting them, we find the interpretation of the passage to be quite altered. What Epicurus was protesting against was the false supposition that *the greatest misfortunes, nay, even the greatest blessings, befall the wicked by the gift of the gods*. His attack is first on the belief that wicked men are punished by the gods, and then on the still more monstrous belief that, by offerings and so forth, wicked men can win favours from the gods. In this sentence no mention at all is made of the good. But in the concluding sentence (the bearing of which is altered if we drop Gassendi's interpolation) what Epicurus really says is this: " For the *gods*, ever familiar with their own virtues, receive men like unto themselves, and reject as alien all that are not of this kind." In other words the notorious indifference of the gods is shown only towards wicked men, whose sole punishment is to be rejected as alien to the divine nature. But good men the gods " receive."

It is commonly believed, in circles where the Epicureans are regarded as atheists in disguise, that it was they who originated and spread the doctrine expressed by Statius in the well-known line:—

" Primus in orbe deos fecit timor."[15]

It is obvious, in the light of what has already been said, that this view of Epicureanism cannot be true, and its falsity has recently been exposed by the careful analysis of Heuten in the Belgian periodical *Latomus* (I. i, Jan., 1937). The Epicureans really believed in the existence of gods, and did so for the same reason that they believed in the existence of other material objects. They thought that they perceived them " by clear vision," to use their own phrase. But this does not exhaust the content of their belief on this point. Only men whose hearts are pure, they taught, can receive truly the images that stream from the divine presences. In their entry into the minds of wicked men these images are distorted and beget false conceptions of the nature of the gods. From these a true philosophy can save us.

The fundamental error, as Lucretius expounds it in his fifth book (1161–1240), is the ascription to the gods of the processes of nature. It is an error to suppose either that the benevolent power of the gods maintains and controls the regular operations of nature, or that such irregular violences as storms, earthquakes, and disease are manifestations of their wrath. Fear did not make the gods; but false ideas of the gods create fear. And this ungrounded fear is responsible for the spread of a false religion among men. To quote, it is this fear that " has spread over great nations the worship of the divinities of the gods and filled towns with altars and led to the performance of stated sacred rites, rites now in fashion on solemn occasions and in solemn places." And this fear propagates itself, for from these sacred rites "even now is implanted in mortals a shuddering awe which raises new temples of the gods over the whole earth and prompts men to crowd them on festive days."

Clearly the Epicureans were spreading the dangerous democratic doctrine that God does not dwell in a temple made with hands—even if the authority responsible for its erection be the State, if the contract for its erection has legally been given to the man who made the lowest tender or had the most influence, and if thousands of slaves have toiled to build it. The Epicureans were so little impressed with all this that they thought that the gods would be quite happy without the reek of incense, the smoke of sacrifice, or the blood of bulls. They also thought that *men* would be much happier if they understood the superfluity of all this. Hence the necessity for a comprehensive doctrine *de rerum natura*. Hence the teaching of Epicurus himself in the *Letter to Herodotus* :—

> "Furthermore, the motions of the heavenly bodies and their turnings and eclipses and risings and settings, and kindred phenomena to these, must not be taught to be due to any being who controls and ordains or has ordained them and at the same time enjoys perfect bliss together with immortality. . . . Nor again must we believe that they, which are but fire agglomerated in a mass, possess blessedness while voluntarily taking upon themselves these movements. Rather must we preserve the majestic significance of all expressions, such as blessedness, which we apply to our conceptions of the gods, in order that there may not arise out of them opinions contrary to the notion of their majesty. Otherwise. this very contradiction will cause the greatest disturbance in men's souls." [16]

Souls thus disturbed, according to Epicurus, were debarred from communion with, and true knowledge of, God. The doctrine on this point is expounded at length by Lucretius in his sixth book (ll. 56–79):—

> "For they who have been rightly taught that the gods lead a life without care, if nevertheless they wonder on what plan all things are carried on, above all in regard to those things which are seen overhead in the ethereal borders, are borne back again into their old religious scruples and take unto themselves hard taskmasters, whom they, poor wretches, believe to be almighty, not knowing what can, what cannot be, in short on what principle each thing has its power defined, its deep-set boundary mark; and therefore they are led all the farther astray by blind reason. Now unless you drive from your mind with loathing all these things, and banish far from you belief in things degrading to the gods and inconsistent with their peace, then often will the holy deities of the gods, having their majesty lessened by you, do you hurt; not that the supreme power of the gods can be so outraged, that in their wrath they shall resolve to exact sharp vengeance, but because you will fancy to yourself that they, though they enjoy quiet and calm peace, do roll great billows of wrath; nor will you approach the sanctuaries of the gods with a calm breast nor will you be able with tranquil peace of mind to take in those idols which are carried from their holy body into the minds of men, as heralds of their divine form. And what kind of life follows after this may be conceived." (It is described in bk. III, ll. 978–1023.)

That this effort of Epicurus, not to destroy belief in the gods, but to purify it, made a profound effect on more orthodox pagan thinkers can be shown by many examples. Perhaps the single most interesting example, which I choose because it shows the persistence of the force of the Epicurean criticism after so many hundred years, is in the tractate of Sallustius [17] *On the Gods*, which Nock in his edition dates A.D. 363. In the ninth chapter, in which he seeks to establish the reign of Providence throughout the universe, Sallustius feels that the Epicurean criticism is still that which he must explicitly meet:—

> "All this care of the world, we must believe, is taken by the gods without any act of will or labour. As bodies which possess some power produce their effects by merely existing: *e.g.*, the sun gives light and heat by merely existing: so, and far more so, the providence of the gods acts without effort to itself and for the good of the objects of its forethought. This solves the problem of the Epicureans, who argue that what is divine neither has trouble itself nor gives trouble to others." (Translation by Gilbert Murray in *Five Stages of Greek Religion*.)

And in his fourteenth chapter, in which he seeks to resolve the problem, *In what sense the gods, though they never change, can be said to be made angry and to be appeased*, Sallustius simply repeats the Epicurean theology with the addition of a belief in devils:—

> "It is impious to suppose that the Divine is affected for good or ill by human things. The gods are always good and always do good and never harm, being always in the same state and like themselves. The truth simply is that, when we are good, we are joined to the gods by our likeness to them; when bad, we are separated from them by our unlikeness. And when we live according to virtue we cling to the gods, and when we become evil we make the gods our enemies— not because they are angered against us, but be-

cause our sins prevent the light of the gods from shining upon us, and put us in communion with spirits of punishment."

If the Epicureans, then, are not responsible for the doctrine that the gods are the product of fear, but teach rather that the gods truly exist and are wholly good, while it is an erroneous belief as to their true nature which has covered the world with temples and introduced religions everywhere, the question arises whether they looked upon this mistaken fear of the gods as a spontaneous product of human weakness, or whether they recognized the existence of some agency which deliberately originated and fostered this fear.

The theory that religion was a political invention had found expression in Greece long before the time of Epicurus. Plato's contemporary, Isocrates, is well acquainted with this view of religion;[18] but the most complete expression it received was from Plato's uncle, the cynical oligarch Critias, in his play of *Sisyphus*. His view was that, since legal punishments could reach only open violence and were powerless to restrain wrongdoers who could elude detection, some shrewd legislator had introduced into the world the belief in all-knowing gods whom no deed, or word, or thought, however secret, could escape. "And he taught," says Critias, "that the gods dwell where he supposed men would be most frightened to believe they dwelt, in the vault above our heads, whence comes our help or our undoing, the brightness of sun, moon, and stars, or the rumble of thunder, the gentle rain, or the crushing thunderbolt. Thus, in my opinion, did a man first persuade mortals that there was a race of gods."

This view, common in the eighteenth century of our own era, was too naïve for the Epicureans. They had too much historical sense to suppose that some imaginary legislator could invent such a system and impose it upon his fellows. Instead, as we have seen from Lucretius, holding that the gods really exist, they taught that the connection of the violences of nature with these divine beings is a natural error, into which the mind of man will easily fall unless fortified with a true philosophy. But while they thus rejected the theories either that fear created the gods or that it was mere policy that taught man the fear of them, they were certainly not strangers to the view that it might be the interest of certain persons to exploit this natural fear. In their self-appointed task of freeing men from superstition they expected opposition. They knew that they were attacking not only an error, but a lie. Thus in the first book of the *De Rerum Natura*, at the close of the great onslaught on *religio*, Lucretius addressing Mummius, proceeds:—

> " You yourself some time or other overcome by the terror-speaking tales of the seers will seek to fall away from us. Ay indeed, for how many dreams may they imagine for you, enough to upset the calculations of life and trouble all your fortunes with fear! And with good cause; for if men saw that there was a fixed limit to their woes, they would be able in some way to withstand the religious scruples and threatenings of the seers. As it is, there is no way, no means of resisting, since they must fear after death everlasting pains."

Here, of course, there is room for speculation as to the identity of these upholders of the religion of fear, these *vates* (seers or priests) whose interests are threatened by the new theology of Epicurus. And, as everywhere in Lucretius, the question may be raised whether we are dealing with a phenomenon of Roman life or with a reference to Greek conditions slavishly repeated from the writings of Epicurus. Since it is a common opinion that the attack on *religio* and on the doctrine of punishments in the after-life is all transcribed from Epicurus, refers to conditions in Greece two hundred years earlier, and has no relevance to the Rome of Lucretius' own day, and since this judgment, if it were true, would affect our whole opinion of Lucretius and his work, it is essential to examine it with some care.

Now, in the opinion of Polybius,[19] who ought to have known what he was talking about, it was precisely to the inculcation of the two errors most strongly combated by Epicurus and Lucretius after him, fear of the gods and belief in the after-life, that the Roman State owed the superiority he claimed for it. " I will venture the assertion," he says, " that what the rest of mankind deride is the foundation of Roman greatness, namely superstition. This element has been introduced into every aspect of their private and public life, with every artifice to awe the imagination, in a degree which could not be improved upon. Many possibly will be at a loss to understand this; but my view is that it has been done to impress the masses. If it were possible to have a State in which all the citizens were philosophers, perhaps we might dispense with this sort of thing. But the masses in every State are unstable, full of lawless desires, of irrational anger, and violent passion.[20] All that can be done, then, is to hold them in check by fears of the unseen and other shams of the same sort. It was not for nothing, but with deliberate design, that the men of old introduced to the masses notions about the gods and concepts of the after-life. The folly and heedlessness are ours, who seek to dispel such illusions." (Polybius, VI, 56.)

We have here a testimony to the Roman practice of exploiting the proneness of ignorant men to superstition with a view to the maintenance of order in a class-divided State. The device which Critias had supposed to have been invented in some distant past by a shrewd legislator is described by Polybius as being in full operation, on an improved model, in the Rome of the second century. Why then suppose that the source of Lucretius' distress is to be sought in books describing conditions in Greece in the fourth century?

I am not unaware that in his latest discussion of Epicureanism at Rome [21] Dr. Cyril Bailey dismisses this evidence of Polybius as inadmissible because unsupported by other testimony to the like effect, and assures us, on the evidence of Cicero, that fears of the after-life were all but unknown in the Rome of Lucretius. His conclusion is that Lucretius took over from Epicurus the whole of his polemic against the fear of torments in the after-life, and "in his slightly abnormal state of mind it became an obsession." Lucretius, therefore, so far from being the liberator of the minds of his fellow men was the solitary dupe in his society of the exploded superstitions of another epoch and another land. With this conclusion I disagree *in toto*, but I am so conscious of being Dr. Bailey's pupil in these matters that I am content merely to call in a champion to support the contrary opinion.

Franz Altheim, in his latest book,[22] passes in review again the great polemic of Lucretius against religion, and then proceeds:—

> "In this polemic we see as in a mirror all that we have seen to be characteristic of the last century of the Republic. We meet the procession of the Mother of the gods to the sound of orgiastic ravings and dances (2,600 f.), we meet the Pythagorean, Ennius, with his dream of Homer; there, too, we meet again all the restless curiosity of the age that was directed towards the beyond and the future destinies of the soul. All this is seen and attacked under the specifically Roman form of *religio*—the Roman and Italian tinge is scarcely ever wanting, whether it be question of the *parentatio* with the sacrifice of black bulls (3, 51 f.), or the description of the grim punishments of hell, in which the walls of the Etruscan

grave-chambers are so rich. Cicero did not disdain to pour the streams of his chill ridicule on a school that praised its founder as the deliverer from dreads in which scarcely any old woman still believed (Tuscul. I, 48). From the standpoint of the Roman nobility, that banished all such elements from *religio* into *superstitio* or passed them over in philosophic enlightenment, this might seem justifiable enough. But what Lucretius aimed at hitting and did indeed hit was that world of Oriental deities, of belief in the beyond, and those magical practices that had their sure and unshakable seat, if not among the nobility, in the middle and lower classes of the population. That the genuine popular belief of Rome itself was not unfamiliar with the conception of ghostly and destructive powers of hell, of their grotesque monsters and the like, has been proved by an investigation of the Mother of the Lares."

It is, indeed, to this difference in outlook between the nobility and the middle and lower classes that we must look if we are to understand the position of Epicureanism at this time in Italy, and Cicero's reaction to it. For though Epicureanism certainly numbered among its adherents at this time many who ranked among the ruling class—Cicero himself had a dozen such men among his friends—it was not their brand of Epicureanism that Cicero feared. It was rather the Epicureanism which had spread among the little people, conveyed in writings which Cicero despised because of their popular style, and had carried all Italy by storm. Why Cicero should fear this we shall consider in a moment. First let us try to make some picture to ourselves of what the effect of Epicureanism as a solvent of superstition among the masses might be. Here I can offer no better evidence than those passages from Lucian's brilliant exposure of the oracle-monger Alexander of Abonouteichus, in which he describes the clash between the impostor and the Epicureans. Alexander, taking the whole of the Empire for his province, had reaped a rich harvest for himself by the sale of his oracles to the superstitious inhabitants not only of the East but of Italy itself, when the opposition, under the leadership of the Epicureans, began to organize itself. "A time came," Lucian tells us, "when a number of sensible people began to shake off their intoxication and combine against him, chief among them the numerous Epicureans; in the cities, the imposture, with all its theatrical accessories, began to be seen through. . . . Well, it was war to the knife between him and Epicurus, and no wonder. What fitter enemy for a charlatan who patronized miracles and hated truth than the thinker who had grasped the nature of things and was in solitary possession of the truth? As for the Platonists, Stoics, Pythagoreans, they were his good friends; he had no quarrel with them. But the unmitigated Epicurus, as he used to call him, could not but be hateful to him, treating all such pretensions as absurd and puerile. . . . In this connection Alexander once made himself supremely ridiculous. Coming across Epicurus' *Accepted Maxims*, the most admirable of his books, as you know, with its terse presentment of his wise conclusions, he brought it into the middle of the market-place, there burned it in a fig-wood fire for the sins of its author, and cast its ashes into the sea. He issued an oracle on the occasion:—

'The dotard's maxims to the flame be given.'

The fellow had no conception of the blessings conferred by that book upon its readers, of the peace, tranquillity, and independence of mind it produces, of the protection it gives against terrors, phantoms, and marvels, vain hopes and inordinate desires, of the judgment and candour that it fosters, or of its true purging of the spirit, not with torches and squills and such rubbish, but with right reason, truth, and frankness." [23]

This picture is drawn from the second century of our era, but we have no reason to suppose that, so far as it goes, it misrepresents the character of Epicureanism as a mass movement in the time of Cicero and Lucretius. And if we here see Epicureans engaged in a struggle against the propagation of superstition through the agency of a private individual, we have to ask ourselves what their attitude must have been to the propagation of superstition by government on the Roman model as described by Polybius. That the possibility of a vigorous resuscitation of government by superstition had begun to be agitated among the nobility at this time is, I think, beyond question. In the struggle between the patricians and the plebeians in the old days religion had always been the second line of defence. Ejected from their monopoly of the civil magistracies, the patricians had entrenched themselves in the priesthoods, and these they had exploited in ever-increasing degree for political purposes. And now, as the Republic staggered to its end, the possibility of a reorganization of the State on a conservative basis, with religion playing a leading rôle, began to present itself. The Stoic teachers, who from the days of the Scipionic circle (middle of the second century B.C.) had been so intimately associated with the governing class in Rome, had familiarized statesmen with their analysis of religion into three parts—political, mythical, and natural. A hundred years later, at about the time when death interrupted Lucretius in the midst of his exposition of the Epicurean view of things, the Stoic influence, which had long fertilized the Roman mind, was bearing rich fruit in the production of the last sixteen books of Varro's *Antiquitates Rerum Humanarum et Divinarum*, in which the knowledge of their religious past was restored to the Romans and the useful function of what Plato called the " noble lie " brought again to their notice. And in the same years Cicero produced the *Republic* (begun in 53 B.C.) and the *Laws* (begun two years later). In these two books, with their Platonic titles and largely Platonic inspiration, the technique of the control of the State through religion is set out with great candour. Life, public and private, is to be involved in a network of religious observances. Priesthoods are to be kept in the hands of the aristocracy. The people, ignorant as to the procedure and rites suitable to these public and private observances, are to seek instruction from the priests. And the reason for this system of laws is frankly given: "the people's constant need for the advice and authority of the aristocracy holds the State together." [24]

It is now surely easy to see how Cicero might, in a private letter in the year 54 B.C., hail with enthusiasm the merits of the *De Rerum Natura* while being unwilling a few years later to acknowledge acquaintance with it in public. The intention of the two great writers is diametrically opposed. With burning sincerity, and in prophetic tones, Lucretius denounces the view of life which Cicero has found it politic to advocate. Probably Cicero did not at once realize how profound their divergence was. He was more intimate, and more at home, with Epicureans of the type of Atticus, and he knew how easily philosophical attitudes could with most men be accommodated to expediency. Atticus might have doubts about the reality of the power of the augurs to ascertain the will of heaven. But augurs as an instrument of class domination are a different thing; and Cicero knows how to banish any hesitation about the desirability of public decisions in a well-ordered State being left to the ratification of these sacred officers. In the idyllic setting of the dialogue of the *Laws*, Cicero and Atticus exchange compliments on the vast size and the numerous amenities of their respective estates, and Cicero profits by the occasion to remind his friend that, but for the ability of the augurs to spike popular legislation, such estates would long ago have been broken up under the operation of agrarian reforms.[25]

Thus while Lucretius was imploring men not to "stain their minds with foul religion," and doing so in close reference to that very cult of the Mother of the Gods which the Roman senate had introduced,[26] Cicero was descanting upon another theme:—

> "So in the very beginning we must persuade our citizens that the gods are the lords and rulers of all things, and that what is done is done by their will and authority; that they are likewise great benefactors of man, observing the character of every individual, what he does, of what wrong he is guilty, and with what intentions and with what piety he fulfils his religious duties; and that they take note of the pious and of the impious. For surely minds which are imbued with such ideas will not fail to form true and useful opinions."[27]

The comment of Gibbon on this legislation is worth quoting: "After the example of Plato," he writes, "he (Cicero) composed a Republic; and for the use of his Republic, a treatise of laws, in which he labours to deduce from a celestial origin the wisdom and justice of the Roman constitution. The whole universe, according to this sublime hypothesis, forms one commonwealth; gods and men, who participate of the same essence, are members of the same community; reason prescribes the law of nature and nations; and all positive institutions, however modified by accident or custom, are drawn from the rule of right, which the Deity has inscribed on every virtuous mind. From these philosophical mysteries, he mildly excludes the sceptics who refuse to believe, and the Epicureans who are unwilling to act. The latter disdain the care of the Republic: he advises them to slumber in their shady gardens. But he humbly intreats that the New Academy should be silent, since her bold objections would too soon destroy the fair and well-ordered structure of his lofty system."[28] So much for Gibbon's judgment on the sincerity of Cicero.

It may be asked whether Gibbon is wholly justified in the use of the phrase: "the Epicureans who are unwilling to act." Those who had shady gardens, privately or collectively, might indeed be invited to slumber in them. But there must have been many who had none. And though the Epicureans might advocate withdrawal from the corrupt life of the State, how far, in fact, did their inactivity go? And if it was possible for Epicurus and his friends in the original Garden to forget the Athens of Demetrius Poliorcetes, how far was it possible for Lucretius, in his time and in his circumstances, to forget the Rome of Cicero and Catiline, of Pompey and Caesar?

Paul Nizan, in his useful book,[29] puts forward the view of two Russian scholars, Bandek and Timosko, which I have not been able to examine at first hand. They contend that there is no justification for regarding Lucretius as a writer indifferent to the life of the city, and they urge that since, according to Varro, religion is a State enterprise, the attack of Lucretius against the gods is a political attack. This position seems to me incontrovertible. I am convinced that Lucretius wrote straight into the heart of a contemporary situation; devoted Epicurean as he was, the doctrine of his master was not the whole furniture of his mind; it was but the sponge which wiped the gum from his eyes so that he might see the world about him, the sword with which he went forth to do battle in it. It was to the sons of Aeneas that, from the first word of his poem, he addressed himself; theirs were the blind hearts whose errors he deplored; theirs would be the victory over *religio* which would put them on a level with the sky. But that one can go beyond this, as Nizan seems inclined to do, and regard him as in any sense the conscious and accepted spokesman of a popular movement, I see no proof. If he was acquainted with the works of his predecessors in turning Epicurean philosophy into Latin, he was as contemptuous of them as was Cicero, for he emphatically claims to be the very first man capable of translating the teachings of Epicurus into Latin [30] and calls attention to his pioneering work in introducing the system to Roman readers and his difficulties in creating a technical vocabulary. His sympathies embraced every class; but he was an intellectual aristocrat and addressed himself to the restricted circle of those who could appreciate a philosophical poem in the purest idiom of the governing class at Rome. If his work came to be distasteful to this class, it was not because of any demagogic element in its appeal—the wider public already had their Amafinius, their Rabirius, their Catius, and the rest—but because in their own idiom it discounted all their values and exposed the hypocrisy of their State.

Certain conclusions would seem to follow with some certainty from these considerations. When ancient writers, as for instance Cicero and Plutarch, charge Epicurus and his followers with atheism, it was not because they were unacquainted with the theology of Epicurus (which among the innumerable theological follies of antiquity was not the most foolish), but because the Epicurean religion could not perform what was for them an essential function of religion. Gods who took no heed whatever of bad men were useless to police the State.

It seems, further, that Epicureanism was an active propagandist creed, and that the direct object of its attack was that aspect of religion which the State thought wise to encourage. To say that the appeal of its champions was to the sensual passions of the mob is mere calumny. On the contrary, the emphasis was on the physical theories of Epicurus; in other words, the effort was directed to the destruction of the belief in the gods of the State, in their essential State function, by the inculcation of the materialist doctrine of atomism. This is the picture as Plutarch paints it in his attack on the Epicurean Colotes

(I quote the lively old version of Philemon Holland):—

> "This (religion) it is that constraineth and holdeth together all humane society, this is the foundation, prop, and stay of all Laws, which they (*i.e.*, the Epicureans) subvert and overthrow directly, who go not round about the bush, as they say, not secretly and by circuit of covert speeches, but openly and even at the first assault set upon the principal point of all, to wit, the opinion of God and Religion."

Plutarch, of course, was a staunch supporter of the Platonic conception of religion.

Here it is of interest to note a contradiction to the usual picture painted of the religious scene in ancient Rome. That picture generally shows an enlightened State struggling to stem the tide of Oriental superstition that welled up from the motley populace below. But here was a powerful movement of rationalism spreading from below, carrying Italy by storm, as Cicero said. And its reception was as cold among the governing class as it was enthusiastic outside it.

The fact is—and this is the dominant fact in the whole situation—that it was the Government itself that was the great purveyor of superstition in ancient Rome. We have heard Polybius, who was the champion of this policy, proclaim it with enthusiastic approval. Six hundred years later, St. Augustine, who as a Christian hated it, exposed it with bitter scorn. Let us listen to him for a moment. First he recalls the dictum of the old pontifex Scaevola (who, incidentally, gave Cicero his first lessons in law), that *it is expedient that States should be deceived in the matter of religion.* He then proceeds to paint a picture of the hypocrisy of the ruling class. We see Cicero the augur ridiculing augury; we see Balbus, the spokesman of Stoicism in Cicero's *De Natura*

Deorum, "uttering with a resounding eloquence, in private, opinions on the gods which he would not breathe in a whisper in a public assembly." For this is the essence of St. Augustine's attack. It is not only that the State religion is false, but that it is maintained for the purpose for which Polybius said it was instituted. Why, asks Augustine, did the old Romans spread false ideas of the gods? And he answers his question: "It was done, of course, for no other reason than that it was the business of these statesmanlike and philosophic gentlemen to deceive the people in the matter of religion, and in so doing not only to set up the worship of devils but to take them as their examples, for the chief delight of devils is deceiving. Devils cannot take possession of men until they have deceived them; so the leaders of the State, who were assuredly not just men but rather devilish, persuaded the people in the name of religion to accept as true what they knew to be lies, thus binding them the more tightly to their form of society so that they might subdue and possess them." So of Varro we read that he betrays clearly enough his conviction that, in his threefold division of religion, only the opinions of the philosophers have any claim to truth, but he restricts all teaching of their doctrines to the four walls of the schools and will not have a word of them uttered in the market-place.

Varro, it is true, attempted to maintain some distinction between the myths of the poets and the teachings of the priests. Augustine will have none of it. "If the poets give Jove a beard, do not the priests the same?" "If Apollo is a harpist on the stage, is he not so at Delphi?" The uneasy pretence which Varro tried to keep up, Seneca felt free to drop. He makes no distinction in essence, but only in function, between the religion of the poets and that of the State. What went on in the temple was, in truth, but what went on on the stage. But "what Seneca felt free to write, he was not free to live." In truth the temple services were lower than the plays of the theatre. At such solemnities, taught Seneca, a philosopher should share in the State ritual, but not let it touch the religion of his heart. "These observances a philosopher will maintain because they are imposed by the law, not because they please the gods." "The whole base throng of gods assembled by a superstition coeval with time we must worship, without forgetting that we do so to set an example, not because they exist." St. Augustine comments: "Philosophy had made him free, but since he was a distinguished senator of the Roman people, he worshipped what he rejected, acted what he condemned, adored what he despised." [31]

St. Augustine certainly would not have approved of the Epicureans. But there was much that united both schools, for both revolted from the hideous hypocrisy of the ancient religion of the State. Hence they were regarded with a common disapproval by the State and by such vulgar charlatans as Alexander the Oracle-monger. "'If there be any atheist or Christian or Epicurean here spying upon our rites, let him depart in haste,' Alexander used to proclaim at the opening of the celebration of his mysteries. 'Christians avaunt,' he would intone, and the crowd responded, 'Epicureans avaunt.' Then was presented the child-bed of Leto and the birth of Apollo, the bridal of Coronis, etc., etc." [32] These proceedings were adopted, we are told, with an eye to his Italian propaganda. Alexander the Oracle-monger knew his public. But of course he was only an amateur at what was, as Augustine put it, the Government's job.

References

[1] Translations from the *Tusculans* are by J. E. King (Loeb Library).

[2] "Cicero hated and despised Epicureanism most sincerely, and one of his chief aims in undertaking his philosophical works was to stem the tide of its popularity in Italy." Reid, *Academica*, Intro., p. 22.

[3] *The Roots of the Tree*, by Carleton Stanley. O.U.P., 1936, pp. 78 ff.

4 Ad Fam XV, 16, i and 19, ii.
5 Wrote on Epicureanism in Latin prose.
6 X, I, 124, *In Epicureis levis quidem sed non iniucundus tamen auctor est Catius.*
7 Reid, *Academica*, Intro., p. 21.
8 See *De Vita et Moribus Epicuri*, bk. III, chap. vi: *De magnis viris in Epicurum non ex rei veritate, sed ex vulgari opinione scribentibus, ac speciatim de Cicerone.*
9 *E.g.*, Fowler, *Religious Experience of the Roman People*, chap. xvi. Bailey, *Phases in the Religion of Ancient Rome*, chap. vii.
10 *Op. cit.*, bk. IV, chap. iii.
11 Plutarch, *adv. Colot.* 31; Cicero *de Nat. Deor* i, cc. 43, 44.
12 The dates of Bailey's studies are: Translation of the *De Rerum Natura*, 1910; edition of the remains of Epicurus, 1926; *Greek Atomists and Epicurus*, 1928; *Phases in the Religion of Ancient Rome*, 1932.
13 *E.g.*, by Hadzsits, *Lucretius and his Influence*, 1935, and by Nizan, *Les Matérialistes de l'Antiquité*, 1936; also, if I am not mistaken, by their reviewers in the English-speaking world.
14 Weidmannsche Buchhandlung, Berlin. It is, of course, not necessary to defend all Jensen's restorations of this charred scroll. All the conclusions from the letter of Epicurus used in this essay were confirmed by Jensen through analysis of familiar Epicurean texts.
15 It was fear that first made gods in the world.
16 Bailey's version, slightly modified.
17 Sallustius was, it seems, a friend of the Emperor Julian, and his treatise is connected with the restoration of paganism.
18 *Busiris*, §§ 24–7.
19 The Greek statesman Polybius, brought to Rome as a hostage in 166 B.C. and retained there for seventeen years, was filled with admiration for Roman ways. His history is far the most illuminating document we possess on its period.
20 This is Plato's doctrine in the *Republic*. He divided the soul into three parts—reason, courage, and appetite—and assigned reason to the senate, courage to the police, and appetite to the masses.
21 *Phases in the Religion of Ancient Rome*, pp. 218–21.
22 *A History of Roman Religion*, pp. 333, 334.
23 Lucian, *Alexander the Oracle-monger*, §§ 25 and 47. Translation by H. W. and F. G. Fowler.
24 *Laws*, chap. ix.
25 *Laws*, II, §§ 6, 7, 13, 14.
26 *De Rerum Natura*, II, 600–60.
27 *Laws*, II, § 15.
28 *Decline and Fall*, chap. xliv. Warde Fowler, who had a more innocent mind than Gibbon, remarks: " It was most fortunate for Rome that her best and ablest men in the second

century fell into the hands, not of Epicureans, but of Stoics."
Op. cit., p. 362.

[29] *Les Matérialistes de l'Antiquité*, 1936, p. 54.
[30] *De Rerum Natura*, V, 336, 337.
[31] The quotations from St. Augustine are from the *de Civitate Dei*, iv, 27, 30, 32; vi, 5, 10.
[32] Lucian, *op. cit.*, § 38.

ALPHABETICAL LIST OF IMPORTANT PERSONS MENTIONED IN THE TEXT, WITH DATES AND OTHER PARTICULARS

Agis, reforming king of Sparta, middle of 3rd century B.C.
Alcmaeon, of Croton, Pythagorean philosopher and pioneer of anatomy, end of 6th century B.C.
Amafinius, translator into Latin and popularizer in Italy of the writings of Epicurus. Earlier than Cicero.
Anacharsis, 6th century Scythian wise man and inventor.
Anaximander, 6th century philosopher of Miletus.
Anaximenes, disciple and associate of Anaximander.
Archimedes, greatest mathematician and engineer of antiquity. A Greek of Syracuse, killed on capture of the town by the Romans, 212 B.C.
Aristotle, philosopher and scientist, 384–322 B.C. Founder of the Lyceum at Athens.
Atticus, wealthy Roman Epicurean, friend of Cicero.
Augustine (Saint), A.D. 354–430, Bishop of Hippo in N. Africa.
Augustus, first Emperor of Rome, ruled 27 B.C.–A.D. 14.

Blossius, of Cumae in Campania, distinguished Stoic philosopher, friend and adviser of Tiberius Gracchus.

Catius, translator into Latin and popularizer in Italy of the writings of Epicurus. Earlier than Cicero.
Celsus, Latin encyclopaedist, flourished A.D. 30, author of the best extant ancient text-book on medicine.
Cicero, Roman orator and philosopher, 106–43 B.C., who in a few years of rapid writing produced a "whole library" of philosophical works teaching an amalgam of Platonism with the doctrines of the Middle Stoic school. His hope was to dislodge the Latin translators of Epicurus. It was largely fulfilled. The writings of Amafinius, Catius, and others have perished.
Cleanthes, of Assos in the Troad, flourished 264 B.C. Called the second founder of Stoicism.
Cleomenes, revolutionary king of Sparta who took up and carried through the work of Agis.
Copernicus, one of the founders of modern astronomy. His work on *The Revolution of the Heavenly Bodies* appeared in 1543.

Democritus, of Abdera, 5th century, founder of atomic system.

IMPORTANT PERSONS MENTIONED 117

Diodorus, of Sicily, Greek author of a "Universal History," born about 90 B.C.

Empedocles, 5th century Greek philosopher of Akragas in Sicily.
Ennius, early Latin epic poet, 239–169 B.C.
Epicurus, founder of Epicurean school, known as the Garden, at Athens, 341–270 B.C.
Erasistratus, Greek anatomist, Alexandrian school, early 3rd century B.C.
Eupalinus, of Megara, 6th century engineer.
Eusebius, father of ecclesiastical history, A.D. 264–340.

Galen, greatest of Greek physicians after Hippocrates. A voluminous writer whose works held the field till after Vesalius.
Gassendi, 1592–1655, restorer of Epicurean studies in modern times.
Glaucus, of Chios, 6th century technician.

Hammurabi, King of Babylon, flourished 2100 B.C.
Heraclitus, of Ephesus, Ionian philosopher, flourished 500 B.C.
Herodotus, of Halicarnassus, historian of the struggle of the Greeks against the Persians, came to Athens 445 B.C.
Herophilus, Greek anatomist, Alexandrian school, early 3rd century B.C.
Hippocrates, of Cos, father of Greek medicine, about 460–380 B.C.
Holland, Philemon, famous Tudor translator of Greek and Latin classics, 1551–1636.

Justin Martyr, Christian apologist, martyred A.D. 166.

Leucippus, probably of Miletus, shares with Democritus the credit for the foundation of the atomic system.
Lucian, born A.D. 120 at Samosata on the Euphrates. Voluminous Greek essayist and satirist.
Lucretius, Roman poet of Epicureanism, contemporary of Cicero. His philosophical poem *On the Nature of Things*, which has survived, is one of our chief sources for the knowledge of Epicureanism and ancient natural philosophy in general.

Ovid, Latin elegiac poet, 43 B.C.–A.D. 18.

Parmenides, founder of Eleatic school, about 500 B.C.
Plato, founder of Academy at Athens, 428–348 B.C.
Pliny, Latin encyclopædist, author of *Natural History*, A.D. 23–79.
Plutarch, greatest biographer of antiquity, about A.D 50–120. Wrote *Parallel Lives of Greeks and Romans*.

I

Polybius, Greek historian taken as hostage to Rome in 166 B.C. Became the admiring spectator and historian of spread of Roman power.
Poseidonius, Stoic philosopher of Middle School, about 130–46 B.C.

Ramazzini, 1633–1714, founder of study of occupational diseases.

Seneca, Roman moralist, killed himself by order of Nero, A.D. 65.
Socrates, 469–399 B.C. Athenian philosopher, inspirer of Plato and others.
Soranus, Greek anatomist, flourished about A.D. 120.
Sphaerus, Stoic philosopher, acted as adviser to revolutionary Spartan king Cleomenes.
Statius, Latin poet, died A.D. 96.

Thales, of Miletus, first Greek philosopher, 6th century.
Theodorus of Samos, end of 6th century, one of greatest inventors of antiquity.
Tiberius Gracchus, Roman land reformer killed by Senatorial land-owning rioters in 133 B.C.

Varro, born 116 B.C., known as the most learned of the Romans. Among his many writings were forty-one books on the religious and political life of the Romans from the earliest times.
Vesalius, the founder of modern anatomy. His work on *The Structure of the Human Body* came out in the same year, 1543, as the chief work of Copernicus.
Virgil, 71–19 B.C. His epic on the destiny of Rome, the *Aeneid*, is a work of supreme beauty and interest. In his youth Virgil was a student of Epicureanism and inclined to dismiss miracle from nature and providence from human history, as Lucretius had done. But in the *Aeneid* nature is again the domain of miracle and history of providence. Virgil becomes anti-rationalist, and practices and beliefs of the old Romans, which Varro had viewed as political expedients, are inculcated as necessary and true. Christian writers early recognized in Virgil " a naturally Christian soul "—*anima naturaliter Christiana*—as they recognized in Lucretius an enemy. A comparison of the two poems is of inexhaustible interest for the understanding of the formation of the mind and conscience of Europe. What Gassendi was doing in the 17th century was to ask Europe to consider whether, in letting Virgil's dismissal of Epicureanism and Cicero's triumph over Amafinius and Catius stand so long unchallenged, it was not doing irreparable damage to mind and conscience.

IMPORTANT PERSONS MENTIONED

Vitruvius, wrote a valuable treatise on architecture, mainly drawn from Greek sources, in the age of Augustus.

Xenophon, Greek historian and philosopher, about 400 B.C.

Zeno, of Citium in Cyprus, founder in Athens of the Stoic school, known as the Porch, about 300 B.C.

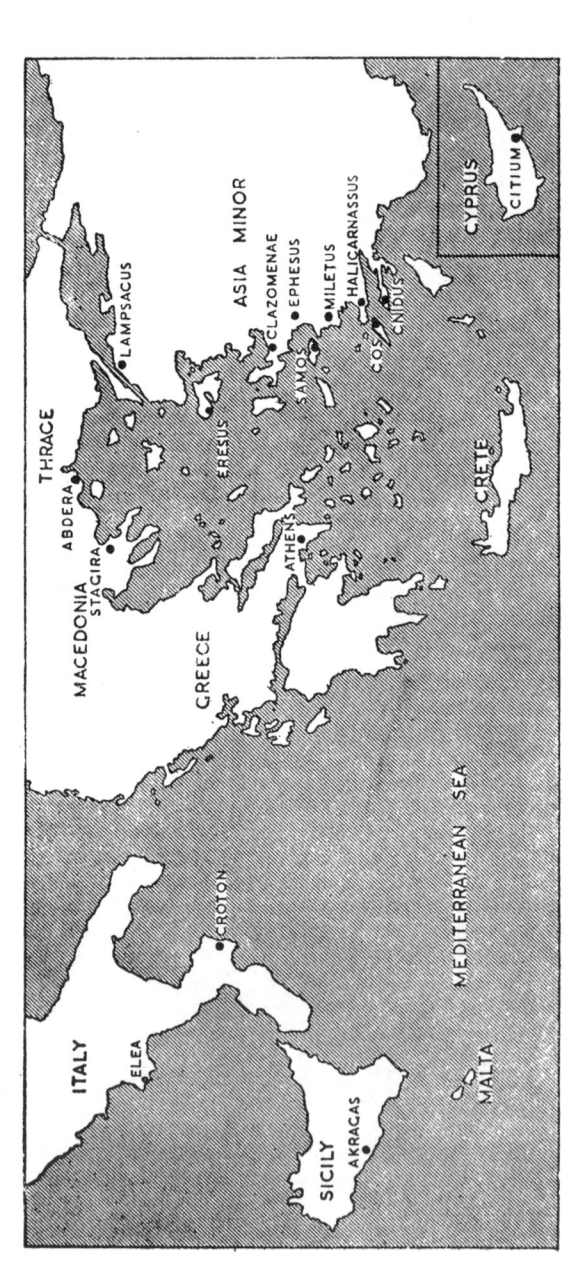

MEN—PLACES—DATES

(To be studied in conjunction with the map)

Greek science began in the town of MILETUS, a cross-roads of the ancient civilizations of the Near East, where colonists of the Ionian branch of the Greeks had settled and intermarried with the older Asiatic population. The Milesians—Thales, Anaximander, and Anaximenes—were the founders of European scientific thought. They flourished from about 585 to 545 B.C. At Miletus also European geography and history began. Anaximander made the first map. The first historian was Hecataeus, who flourished about 500 B.C.

Greek science was not confined to one spot. It was rather a manifestation of the mental development of the Greek people as a whole. Moving south from Miletus we come to HALICARNASSUS. This was the birthplace of the historian Herodotus (about 484–425 B.C.), whose extant history is a typical product of the Ionian enlightenment. But the Dorian Greeks also shared in the movement. A little further south lie the Dorian settlements of COS and CNIDUS. They were the seats of famous medical schools which from about 500 B.C. began to make contributions of fundamental importance to science.

Turning north from Miletus we come to EPHESUS, the home of Heraclitus (flourished about 500 B.C.), and to CLAZOMENAE, from which Anaxagoras (500–428 B.C.) came to the Athens of Pericles. Then on the Dardanelles we find LAMPSACUS, to which Anaxagoras retired on being banished from Athens for impiety, and from which, about one hundred and twenty years later, Epicurus transferred his school to Athens.

Crossing over to Europe we reach ABDERA in Thrace, the home of two famous thinkers—the sophist Protagoras and his younger contemporary Democritus (flourished about 430 B.C.), the founder of the atomic system of philosophy. Further west in Macedonia lies STAGIRA, the birthplace of Aristotle, from which he departed at about the age of seventeen to study under Plato in the Academy at Athens.

Passing over Greece proper and coming to Magna Graecia we should first identify the town of CROTON. It was here that Pythagoras (about 572–500 B.C.), the first philosopher and scientist of Western Europe, set up his school after emigrating from the island of SAMOS. Schools influenced by his teaching soon appeared at ELEA, made famous in the first half of the fifth century by Parmenides and Zeno, and at AKRAGAS in Sicily, the home of Empedocles (flourished about 450 B.C.).

At ATHENS the scientific movement began with Anaxagoras about 450 B.C., and for about one hundred and fifty years its main centre was there. The greatest names are Socrates, Plato, Aristotle, and Theophrastus, who came to Athens from ERESUS in the island of LESBOS. It was just at the close of this period that Epicurus and Zeno founded at Athens the two great philosophical schools which divided the allegiance of the classical world in later centuries. Epicurus, who had been born of Athenian parents in Samos, had established his school at Lampsacus before transferring it to Athens. The founder of Stoicism was a Phoenician merchant from CITIUM in CYPRUS.

After 300 B.C., with the establishment of the Greek dynasty of the Ptolemies in Egypt, ALEXANDRIA, with its library and museum, became the centre of science and learning. Alexandria remained the greatest, though not of course the only, centre of Greek learning until the foundation of Constantinople early in the fourth century A.D.

Socialist Classics

Max Beer: *A History of British Socialism* (£11.95).

Eduard Bernstein: *Cromwell and Communism* (£15.00).

H.N. Brailsford: *The Levellers and the English Revolution*
edited by Christopher Hill (£18.00).

Thomas Spence: *Pigs' Meat —
Selected Writings of a Radical and Pioneer Land Reformer*
(£9.95).

R.H. Tawney: *The Attack* with a foreword by Tony Benn
(£6.95).

N.I. Bukharin: *Selected Writings* (£20.00).

available from
Spokesman Books
Russell House
Bulwell Lane
Nottingham NG6 0BT
phone 0115 9708318
fax 0115 9420 433
e-mail elfeuro@compuserve.com